C000272918

My Life Through An Open Door of Mercy

Introduction by the author Simon Walker

Outside William Wordsworth's Dove Cottage in Grasmere, Cumbria. I have always loved poetry.

Dear Reader, thank you for your interest in this book. The royalties from this publication are going to support children living in poverty, please be generous. Thank you.

I firstly want to share that where human beings close doors in your face, not just physically, Almighty God opens doors that no one can shut in your face. There is a saying I heard as a child: If Almighty God is only your co-pilot you are in the wrong seat! These are wise words from someone that remained anonymous. No doubt inspired by Almighty God Himself. I asked Almighty God to be Chief Pilot of my mind, body, soul and spirit back in 1983 and He has been ever since. Almighty God is the greatest friend I will ever have, and you will ever have and He will always be with you and gracious.

The story you are about to read is an honest account of my life so far, and is nothing less than miraculous. I will tell you about events in my life and Almighty God's part in it all. My life is all founded on the Lord. Unfortunately, I need to speak about the devil and my battles with the evil one. The devil hates those that love Jesus. I will write other things as the Holy Spirit guides me. Most importantly I will write about Almighty God's wonderful love for you. Almighty God has been so gracious and giving of Himself to me, this is no fluke! I will never be able to repay Him or thank Him enough; I know none of us will. It is all His wonderful unconditional grace, but we do need to be reconciled to Him and accept His Beloved Son who died for us all so we can be forgiven. We all need forgiveness for things we have said, done, and failed to do.

I would like to start with a prayer of thanksgiving:

Heavenly Father, in the name of your only begotten Son Our Lord Jesus Christ, I thank you for this opportunity to give you all the praise and all the glory. I thank you for my strength and my health. I thank you for your mercy and grace, I thank you for all the blessings you have given me, and I thank you for the Lord Jesus being my Lord and Saviour. Amen.

For many years I have been inspired and was thinking about writing a book, and for a very long time the title of the book – My Life through an Open Door has been stuck in my mind. The "Of Mercy" has been recently added.

Let me in a few words tell you about Jesus. Many only hear about Him as a swear word. Jesus is so much greater than a swear word. Everything was made through Him and for Him. He came down from heaven and did many wonderful and miraculous things. He died for you and me out of love so we might go to heaven. He rose from the dead and went back to heaven. This is good news and good news should be shared, right?

The Lord Jesus Christ tells us that: **"I stand at the door and knock, if anyone hears my voice and opens the door, I will come in,"** (Revelation 3:20). We must open the door of our lives to the Lord Jesus. He will not violate the free will He has given us. The door handle is on the inside of our lives, and we must be the ones to open the door and invite the Lord Jesus in. The Lord Jesus has promised He will "Give us life to the fullest." (John 10:10). He has certainly given that to me as you will find out in this book about my life so far. My writings are from my heart. Many intellects think polished writing is what matters, if one is writing a novel may be so, but what matters is what is in a person's heart when giving glory to Almighty God.

Still on the topic of doors, St. Ambrose a 4th Century bishop once said: **"Our door is faith; if it is strong enough, the whole house is safe. This is the door by which Christ enters."**

It is very important to always give thanks to Almighty God for His goodness and to bear witness to His love whenever possible. We are never to be afraid if your love for Almighty God even if it does not sit comfortable with others. Almighty God must always come first and there are to be no comparisons with Him (Luke 14:26).

In this book, I wish to do exactly this, give Him all the glory and of course give my upmost thanks to Him. I have been through times that have proved to be very tough. I will share those life experiences to show what Almighty God has done for me, and the way He has helped me. Almighty God's work is nothing short of miraculous. I am writing to give my personal upmost thanks to Him for His goodness to me, and to bear witness to His unfailing love. I personally thank Almighty God for all the prayers that He has listened to and answered. We have so much to thank Him for.

As St. Paul tells us: **"In life, we must run the race as winners until we receive the prize"**

(1 Corinthians 9:24). The race in life might be a difficult one and be different for each of us, but it will be all worth it in the end; for the prize the Lord Jesus Christ will give those who love Him and serve Him: eternal happiness in heaven with Him.

It is my prayerful good wish that I do not throw religion down your throat, but that all who read this book will see Almighty God, not me, and accept, follow and glorify the Lord Jesus Christ and make Him known to others.

Best wishes and prayers, your friend Simon.

I was born on the 18th November 1973 at Crumpsall Hospital now North Manchester General Hospital to poor yet upstanding parents with decency and morals. I could not have been given a better mam and dad in all fairness. Even though despite their hard work we were not wealthy but we were spiritually rich. It was because of my mam and dad that I stayed in school, did not hang around in gangs, had respect for my elders, and did not take drugs. If they had not done their parental duties like many do not do today, I would have no doubt gone down the wrong road.

My parents have told me stories when they were youngsters about their poverty experiences despite both sets of my grandparents working, my grandad Beddow (mam's dad) put cardboard in my mam's shoes because they could not afford a new pair of shoes for her, but once the cardboard was wet they would re-start the process, and my poor dad having to go outside with a candle to use the loo in the early hours, then having to break the ice because the outside loo was frozen solid! All he had to play with was a tin can, no toys! Tough times for those born in that era. It was during this time in the late 1940's early 50's that Great Britain was consider one, if not the richest country in the world, so much for fairness and sharing life's resources. Times were hard for many.

My mam told me I was baptised and made a child of God on the 10th March 1974 in a simple service at Moston Methodist Church. In 1975 when I was nearly two, my brother Paul was born. I said I would need to speak about the devil, this I do reluctantly. It was during the first few years of my life that I had a very horrible experience that I will never forget. I was 3 years old and sat at our front door playing with a toy car on the pavement because the wheels would not turn on the carpet. Two older boys I did not know, I would say about 9 or 10 years, grabbed me by my coat, shouted at me, and dragged me to the alleyway where is was wet and muddy and said: **"If you do not rub mud all over your face we are going to beat you up!"** Of course, I was very frightened and I did as I was told. I started crying believing they would harm me. I can remember seeing evil in their eyes and as I rubbed in my face and they were both laughing and pointing at me. My mam heard me crying, came out, and the boys ran away. My mam had noticed however which house they had ran to from the alleyway and both had entered the same house, looking back they were no doubt close friends or relatives. My mam went with me and spoke with their dad; I stood there covered in mud, but thankfully not injured. I was informed years later from my mam that those boys were disciplined by their dad, and my mam said she heard them both crying as we walked away. It was only later in life through the help of the Holy Spirit that I realised it was the devil himself that had influenced these two lads to behave that way towards me.

That experience will always live with me. The devil hated me and wanted to humiliate me even as a baby. The devil does use children as well as adults to do his work; the killers of baby Jamie Bulger in 1993 are clear evidence of this. When I was about 5 years old a child sat in my class at school, a lad in my class lunged at me for no reason. This caused me to fall back ways on my chair and I banged my head on a very hard radiator. I was taken to hospital and would later suffer in my educational studies. For those that do not know, the devil is Almighty God's enemy; Satan as he is known, is a fallen Angel, cast out of heaven by Almighty God because of pride and disobedience. The devil could not accept the mercy of Almighty God, and His plan for salvation, the devil hates mercy. I promote Almighty God's mercy and he hates me.

Going back to my childhood, in December 1977, my Nana Walker died; I was only age 4 so can recall very little about her, but to this day I can remember once sitting on her knee looking up at her. A very loving and gentle lady. RIP Nana Walker. X

In 1980, as a family we moved from Moston to Chadderton in Oldham. I started at a new school. From what I can call to mind; the years that followed were ordinary, but I remember I enjoyed pushing people's buttons like most kids did I think and getting a reaction for my own amusement, sometimes I would not know when to draw the line until I was rightfully disciplined. It never did me any harm either. I thank my mam and dad for this.

In 1983, my second brother Trevor was born, and that was the year I came to the Almighty; I was 9 years old. Firstly I must share that I remember on one occasion as a young lad, it was on a Saturday morning, I was coming down the stairs before breakfast and the TV was on; it was Tiswas, a lively children's programme hosted by Chris Tarrant, some readers may remember Tiswas. What I saw on that programme affected me for the rest of my life. It was all a mess about and people being stupid. That morning, a man was tied down on a bench and others on the programme were throwing food over him – beans, mushy peas, and custard. This made me literally heave, I think it was because I had not yet had breakfast. I have never ate any of the mentioned foods and do not like seeing them. I did enjoy school meals especially cheese and onion pie, this was usually served on Fridays, was one of my favourites, and there was always plenty left over and the dinner ladies would shout: "Anyone for seconds?" Sometimes thirds were shouted! There needed only to be the one call and the dinner queue was full again. One sad part about school dinners in my case was, there would be usually something I would enjoy, but then mushy peas or beans would be put on my plate even though I did not like it. I would say no thanks but what I did not like was put on my plate ruining my dinner. The dinner ladies must have been instructed to put everything on the plates of students even if it was not liked, this spoilt some of my dinners. It would not have happened today with so many rights for youngsters even those wishing to sue their parents have that right today!

There was another experience at my junior school that was not pleasant for me. A girl accused me of bullying her in the playground and I was brought to the office. I told the teacher that I had not bullied her or anyone because I was always playing football in the school playground at play time. I remember the teacher asking my parents to come in. The teacher said: "It must be your Simon, because he fits the description from the coat he is wearing." I wore a warm blue Parka coat in them days with a fluffy hood.

Anyway, it was decided that I would not be allowed to play out at play time for one full week, and I would need to sit with the head teacher's office every play time. Other students would walk passed me sat there and some would snigger at me. Since then I have never liked being present in offices of people in authority, even if I am not there for negative reasons. Anyway, I was not any wiser at that age, looking back there was the devil again working against me. I remember towards the end of the week the girl reporting again that I had been bullying her in the playground, but how could I have been? I was sitting in the head teacher's office, and the head teacher, he knew it! I missed playing football, but in order to be exonerated from bullying, I suppose it was worth it! It turned out that a lad wearing the same kind of coat was responsible and was eventually caught and dealt with by the teacher. The truth always prevails.

My first encounter with Almighty God came one Sunday evening. I was playing football with my friend David on Asia field in Chadderton (it was always known as the back field to the locals). We had been playing for hours, and were sat on the grass having a rest. David had noticed that there was a church building in the distance with its lights on; I had not really noticed it before, just focused on playing football. David said: "Come on, let's go and see what's going on there." I said: "alright," and followed him. As we approached the church, instead of David who was in front of me walking to where the doors were, he started climbing the church wall at the side so he could look through the window. I followed him, and as I started climbing the wall, I felt a stick across my back pinning me up against the wall. I was trembling and heard a man's voice say: "Come on, get down!!" David said: "Quick run." I noticed that my friend David had ran off and left me (David was much smaller than me, and quicker). As I turned around, I saw an elderly man and with him was an elderly woman.

He said: "This is no way to treat a house of prayer." I was nearly in tears and nervously replied: "I did not mean any harm…., we were just seeing what was going on." I felt very upset, and even more upset that I did not think they believed me. I said: "Sorry," before I was sent on my way, I was asked for my name, and they gave me their names Mr and Mrs Hartley. One evening around two weeks later, I was walking to the shop to buy some sweets; I was near the same church it was called Emmanuel Parish Church, I saw Mrs Hartley again. At first, I could not look at her in the eye, I was embarrassed. Mrs Hartley said: "Hello, how are you?" I said: "Fine, I am really sorry about that Sunday." My apology was accepted, and Mrs Hartley said: "You are very welcome to join us Simon, the Lord Jesus loves everyone." I knew nothing about Jesus, just heard of His name, often used has a swear word, but not at our house. I thought about the invitation, and although I could not make sense of it all said I would attend the church that Sunday evening for the service. I let my parents know who were happy for me to go as the church was only a short walk from our house. I attended the service that Sunday.

I was given a service book, hymn book, and the weekly newsletter. I did not understand any of it really, and I struggled to keep up with the first service I attended. I was told not to worry as I sat next to the Vicar's wife Audrey.

The church that I attended was Emmanuel Parish Church, and the vicar at the time was called the Rev Eric. I started going to church every week and picking things up about the service. I joined the choir within weeks as I loved to sing, and I have always been very fond of music. I was informed by the choir master that to sing to Almighty God was to pray twice a saying also of old from St. Augustine. I wanted this Lord Jesus that the Rev Eric spoke about to come into my life too. I was informed that the Lord Jesus had died for us, and if this was the case, He deserved my commitment, respect and to be a part of my life. I kept asking Him to come into my life. My spirituality became somewhat restless in a short time though. I spoke with the Rev Eric about it who said very gently to me: "Simon, the Lord is already your saviour, you only need to ask Him once, and He can hear you!"

Over the next couple of years, my walk of faith continued; I received from Almighty God in His goodness the seven gifts of the Holy Spirit, in particular discerning the spirits and the gift of healing. I can be in the company of a complete stranger and within a few seconds I can discern whether they have a bad spirit working in them. Sadly many people do, mostly unbelievers, but believers too. A bit later on you will read when I came face to face with the devil himself in the form of snakes working through someone. It sounds bizarre I know, but true. The devil can take many forms.

At age 14, my brother Paul and I got paper rounds; I can remember us traipsing to the paper shop at 6am in our Parka coats with the fluffy hoods up when it was freezing; a fiver for 6 mornings we were paid, and a quid a round on Sundays! Most of the other kids were faster than me so by the time I had finished my round, the other kids had done 2 or 3 rounds on a Sunday! I also did odd jobs during my school years working in shops at weekends for a bit of spending money, this included washing the freezers in a butcher shop, helping a bad tempered green grocer out, including cleaning up after his dog and pups, and working in a shoe shop. My employers certainly got their monies worth out me as they usually do out of most people. I have no regrets earning from the work Almighty God gave me.

I played school boy competitive football in my spare time; that was my best hobby. I owe so much to my beloved dad Kevin who gave his time up to train me, and he who came out on the field with me in rain, sleet or shine; to support me becoming the best I could be. I was a Goalkeeper, and very passionate about keeping the ball from going in the net; at times I would get upset when the ball went in. With my dad's help, I played at town team level for Oldham boys in 1984 for the under 11's and 1987 for the under 14's. I played at the inter league level and considered to be one of the best goalie's in the league – wow! My dad was a great manager of junior teams; I played for his teams through the years, there was never any favouritism, I was told just like the others if I had poor form. My mam and dad took great pride in sending their teams out very smartly; my mam was the backbone of the clubs my dad managed; her duties included washing the muddy kits every week, and she never complained. My parents were also successful in managing winning teams that won various league titles and cups. Looking back, between them they no doubt took hundreds of kids off the streets over the years that would otherwise have been bored, and provided a great provision for only 50p a week! This paid for the rent of the pitch/gym and the players' refreshments, cheap childminders I have heard my mam and dad called. I am very surprised that neither my mam nor dad was publicly recognised for their work in the community, but I know they did not do it for that – honestly. They even put their own money in to keep things running.

I did not just love playing football, I was also involved in other sports, and I loved and still love swimming. In 1985, I started at a new school; "big school." I did not have the best start though; within the first week while in lesson, I was brought out by the teacher in front of the whole maths class to do a sum on the board, and I completely froze because I did not understand what I was being taught, I was trying to listen, but nothing was sinking in. As a result of me not responding, there was silence in the classroom and all eyes were on me. I was shouted at by this well set teacher in front of the whole class of around 30 other kids, most of them I did not know. I was accused of not listening. The maths teacher was very tall, broad and he had thick ginger hair and a thick ginger beard, quite scary looking for a young person to look at to be honest. I felt so humiliated and embarrassed by the way he dealt with me. My school life did not get any better; I went through that school being told by some teachers that I was not trying hard enough; was not concentrating, and was lazy, in my heart I knew this was not true. The other kids in my class were a mix of good and not so good kids and of course there was disruption, this did not help me having difficulty learning. I knew something was not right and I asked for support, but was given very little help at school. It was as if no one had the time, may be they did not have the time, I do not know, there were a lot of other kids to deal with I know.

Because I was on a downer most of the time, I started to resent the system, and became verbally confrontational at times, although not abusive towards people, but nevertheless difficult and stubborn. I was a child, but with an old outlook on my shoulders, but I did not know my place as a minor. I could not wait to become an adult to be honest. I wanted respecting if I was going to give respect. I would often forget I was the minor though. I remember on one occasion in a cooking class the deputy head teacher was present before the class even started, it was true that some kids in my class could not be trusted to cook and behave near a cooker, but I could be trusted. I felt that I was not trusted either, this upset me. Because of all the negativity at school except when in PE, there was tension at home and the negativity reflected on my mam and dad. I remember arguing and get so upset I went to the bathroom, looked at myself in the mirror with tears in my eyes, hating myself and the situation. I remember I was thinking of taking some pills from the cabinet, but I heard a beautiful voice say: "**Don't Simon, I love you**." I listened. If I had not I might not be here today!

In my youth, I had also started to suffer from very bad headaches. I thought it was as a result of banging my head from being pushed off my chair as a toddler, but it was not. My doctor carried out tests and prescribed me with painkillers, but the pain would not go away. The headaches when they came gave me a great discomfort. The best way to describe the pain, it was a burning sensation, causing me to be very tired, and I found it difficult to concentrate on anything especially at school. This was not the obstacle a young person needed. I felt a bit of a failure from the moment that maths teacher singled me out and embarrassed me; I became more stubborn, but in fear because teachers could and did hit you then. I still think about that today, and the way I was humiliated by that maths teacher. I often wondered if I was over reacting, but I do not think I was. I should not have been treated like that and it was alright to be upset. Thanks be to Almighty God for helping me lose the resentment I had towards him. I could not have let go of the resentment I had against that maths teacher without Almighty God's help.

In 1986, I started learning Aikido at my secondary school and trained every Tuesday and Thursday lunchtime. Aikido is a martial art for readers that do not know. Martial arts was a breath of fresh air and something I loved being in school for. Many teachers looked at me in a different way I think and I started to earn respect, and my instructor, a science teacher, liked me. To do martial arts requires discipline and commitment. I know Almighty God guided me in all this and works in wonderful ways. Aikido was something I loved doing. I picked up quickly especially the Japanese names for moves my heart was in Aikido. Not bad for someone who would years later be diagnosed with mild dyslexia. Do forgive therefore any errors in the book please!

In the Old Testament law; limitations are placed on vengeance (Exodus 21:23-25). In Matthew 5:38-48; Jesus implied that we must give up vengeance altogether, however I need to point out that defending oneself, family, friends or in the support of law and order from attack is not vengeance or against Almighty God.

As Christians, we are called the turn the other cheek when possible, and be humble, not to be weak or a door mat to be walked over. Nowhere in the Bible does it say that:

"Blessed are the doormats for they shall inherit the heel." As Christians, we are to be bold and confident with the full armour of Almighty God on us (Ephesians 6:11). To wear armour is to be prepared for battle. We need to be in this pagan world, sadly turning the other cheek these days will result in being hit on the other cheek as well. We are in a battle and should be prepared to go on the offensive if required.

Although the battle primarily applies to our spiritual lives; we must care also for our physical lives too.

The devil is only too eager for an opportunity to harm someone if permitted to do so.

I do not wish to go on a tangent here, but the fact is, if more people learned a martial art, and attackers were on the receiving end of the art of the defence; the attackers would think again about carrying out evil by attacking in order to rob or assault someone. This would make the world a safer place. As a black belt in Aikido, I can verify that it improves fitness and self - confidence.

There are millions of people throughout the world practising Aikido from all walks of life. I would certainly recommend to you the reader to look into learning Aikido and other forms of martial arts.

Randori or Kokyunage as it is often referred to, essentially relies on blending and flowing with your partner's movement and upsetting his/her balance.

In Aikido, it is possible to defend yourself, control your attacker without not always inflicting pain on them. Aikido is also a great way to keep fit and socialise, I have made some great friends over the years and I have been honoured to train with some very experienced instructors.

Morihei Ueshiba 1883 – 1969

The founder of Aikido

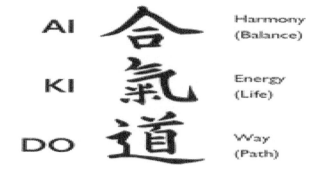

AI   合   Harmony (Balance)

KI   氣   Energy (Life)

DO   道   Way (Path)

My story continues from my teenage years. I did not really like being at school, I found the whole experience frustrating, it was a good job I had my faith and activities, mainly football and Aikido otherwise my time at school would have been very miserable for me. There was very little Christianity in the school; in fact we had just one lesson per week on religious education, and it was difficult to learn with a lot the disruption some the kids in my class did not have any respect for the school, teachers or the system. I had the respect, but I did not want to be in this company and I felt I was painted with the same brush as the others. I did not help myself though and would try and fight the system like many others were. The old saying goes: "I wish I knew then what I know now." As a child, I did lack awareness that my teachers were there to help me, and I would not even consider that my teachers' lives would have been stressful, many no doubt with families and stresses of their own. I could not wait to grow up. In the school assembly we only sung one hymn. I sung, but I would look around, (as often I already knew the hymn from church), and I noticed that the teachers were all lined up at the side of the hall with their different classes, and were not even singing in thanks to Almighty God. The Holy Spirit informed me many teachers did not believe in Him. This I did not like. My attitude at times was confrontational. Looking back, I wish I would have gone to a faith school, but then if there were no other Christians at my school; I would be the only one in a relationship with Almighty God and praying for the school and that could be why I was there, God's will.

I stayed in school because it was my parents' wishes, my love for football in PE, and my love for Aikido. I never took drugs, I was not offered any either thankfully. I loved my football and was chosen to represent my town: Oldham boys under 14's team. We were considered the best players in the town for our age group. It was a pity that the town team only offered under 11's and the under 14's at that time. I was very fortunate enough to represent my town in both years at my junior school and secondary school, under 11's and under 14's. The highlight of my career in football was when I was on the winning teams in cup finals in 1984 playing for Millnote Juniors and with another team managed by my dad in 1987 called Slumberland Rangers. I will never forget playing for my town against Salford boys in a friendly home game, and I played against the Manchester United legend Ryan Giggs. He scored twice passed me; I got my hand to one, but the other was like a bullet, I did not even see it until I was picking it out of the net! We lost the game 0-2.

I attended the football school of excellence for Manchester City, Oldham Athletic, and Rochdale FC, but sadly never made the grade as a professional. I was always told that to become a professional you not only need to be good, but you need a "bit of luck." Luck in the football world was what I did not get when I needed it, thank God I never sustained any injuries. Like so many young lads, I did not make it as a professional! I joined the list of many millions that wanted to become a professional, but it was something I could only dream about. I did train and meet some professional Goalkeepers that I will never forget. Out of all the lads I knew who were playing, only a handful became professional.

In 1988, my dad and I wanted to put something back into the game that had given us so much enjoyment so we decided to become Football Association Referees and we attended a referees' course with the Manchester Football Association. The motto for Referees is "You do not referee to keep fit, you keep fit to referee." A lad I started to pal about with near where we lived said we wanted to join us, but never did. He was older than me and was not a good influence to be honest. I tried cigarettes at his suggestion. I was not very smart though, one evening whilst my non - smoking family were asleep, a lit a cigarette in the living room, but instead of using air fresher, I used furniture polish, I was caught because the smell was easily detected by my parents. I was rightly disciplined, our house was smoke free!

Anyway, my dad and I qualified soon after as F.A referees. We refereed for over 6 years. One occasion about 5 years later after qualifying, I refereed a game, and low and behold who was playing on one team - only my old secondary school teachers, but not my maths teacher. Even then having left school, some of the teachers were still trying to undermine me and treated me like a pupil and swearing on the pitch. But things were different now; I was the ref, I was in charge and with the authority – lucky me! I did not abuse my authority when refereeing, no ref should do, but I needed to have the odd gentle word with one or two of the teachers. After the game both teams shook my hand and said "Thanks Ref, good game." I took the opportunity to ask one teacher a question: "Was I a bad student at school?" He said: "No Simon, you were not a bad lad, there were a lot worse than you, even some of the teachers could have been better." I did not understand what he meant by this, but it was revealed later on to me by The Holy Spirit regards to the conduct of many teachers in my secondary school that in their personal lives some had been involved in extra martial affairs.

My Dad and I were paid £5 per game, and refereed in all weathers - rain, sleet or shine and most pitches in winter were boggy. We were required to pay for our petrol out of that as well, not much left after that. It was a tough job and you needed to have eyes in the back of your head! As a ref, you would only have two assistants when the game was a cup semi-final or a cup final. You would therefore need to give each manager a flag to assist when the ball went in and out of play. Sadly, as a ref, I found that I could not depend or trust many non-officials with the offside rule because I experienced some trying to cheat for their team, flagging for offside when it clearly was not offside, and there would be chaos and a potential trouble between supporters. The job as a ref was therefore made harder. I used my whistle as little as possible and my dad did too. We tried to keep the game flowing. Like all referees you needed to deal with those supporters on the side-lines swearing and shouting abuse even when you thought you were having a good game. On more than one occasion both dad and I would need to send supporters away from the touch line. They would usually go and sit in their cars. Thanks to Almighty God, we did not have to put up with the level of verbal abuse and physical attacks that goes on today, even MP's are calling for more protection for referees because of the amount that are abused and seriously assaulted! Who would think that just trying to do your job could put you in that predicament? I remember an Asian lad, a really good bloke and ref, but he was racially abused and gave it up, he was not going to put up with it for a fiver was he? I can remember on our referees' course, our coach telling us a story about a former professional referee George Courtney, who was in charge of a game in a lower league and as far as he was concerned was going well. But at half time, as George was coming off for his half time cup of tea, he was met by verbal abuse and booed off by loads of fans. He entered the dressing room and apparently said to his assistants: "What have I done wrong lads?" "We do not know, nothing George" was their reply. Refereeing was not an easy job, but very rewarding. Almighty God really helped me when I was refereeing, and I always asked my Guardian Angel to go before me when I was advising or disciplining anyone. I did miss a handball once during a very tense game because a player came across my path and obstructed my view so I could not give a penalty. Some of the players wanted to hang me for not giving it. On two occasions my dad and I went to referee at Pontins holiday place in Morecambe at a football festival. The first time we went was in 1993. I had passed my driving test in 1992, and I had my first car by then. It was a B registration Rover Metro so we went in that. We did not have a Sat Nav then but my dad had the A-Z map. It looked so confusing. My dad used to make me laugh because we would be quite literally on top of the junction when my dad would say: "It is here, turn here." You can imagine what it was like driving no doubt dear reader. Anyway, we were about 1 mile away from the venue looking forward to staying for the week at Pontins, refereeing every day, accommodation and food would be provided, and we was to be paid a fiver per match. As we were approaching the complex on a narrow road we noticed there was a lot of water on the road about 1 foot high, we stopped and wondered if it would go up my exhaust and should we drive through it and take a chance. I took the chance but before I made it right through the water my car just cut out. We rolled out of the water so we could step out the car without getting our feet wet. We were stranded and I did not have any motor rescue cover. We could only wait for someone to pass that was also heading to Pontins. We flagged a lift and a man kindly stopped. He was going to Pontins too. I waited in my car and my dad went with the man to Pontins to sign us in at the tournament and get some help for me. I could only wait in the car; my car battery had life so I listened to the radio and said some prayers. As always and without fail, Almighty God answered. My dad came back about an hour later in another car with a different man. Thank God this man used a rope he had and towed me and my car out of the water and to Pontins.

Anyway, the days went by and my dad was becoming increasingly anxious on how we would get home after the tournament because my car would still not start. I remember saying: "Do not worry dad, the Lord Jesus will look after us." It was the last night before we were set to leave for Manchester. I suppose I should have been panicking but I was not, no credit to me, but all thanksgiving to Almighty God for this. Anyway, we were in the bar and my dad got talking to someone, a complete stranger, someone involved in the tournament, about football and other things. He told him what had happened to us when we arrived and about my car not starting all week after I drove through the water. The man said: "Do not worry, use this, I am covered for any driver." He handed my dad his RAC recovery card. When my dad told me I said: "Praise God." My dad called the RAC out and a mechanic arrived at Pontins to look at my car. The mechanic worked 2 hours solid and got my car started again. This was a miracle from Almighty God. He did not abandon us and always keeps His promises. "And if we know that He hears us, whatever we ask, we know that we have what we asked of Him." (1.John 5:15). Or even more fitting: "The waters may rise, but they will not overtake you." Isaiah 43:2 (I smile). The following year my dad and I went back and refereed again at the tournament. I had a different car then and when we arrived, there was no water on the road. The tournament went well. It was on the way home that Almighty God came to our rescue again. We must have been at least 20 miles from home when my car engine set on fire on the motorway, thanks be to Almighty God we escaped and the fire service arrived and put out the fire before my car blow up. We were stranded again. I prayed, and the motorway recovery truck turned up because my vehicle was in the way and was a distraction because other drivers kept looking at my burnt out car. Anyway, the recovery driver said: "It is OK; I will take you home, no charge." Thanks be to Almighty God again for looking after us. It was only due to starting shift work at the hospital and including working most weekends that refereeing became difficult to continue. I have some regret not continuing refereeing, and who knows I could have refereed a professional game, but it was not to be.

In March 1990, I continued to be frustrated with school and I struggled. It was the year I was due to leave, and my parents and I went to school to ask if I could leave early, find a job and come back in for my exams in May/June 1990. I put my request in, and soon after my Head Tutor for my year called me to the office to answer my request and said: "Simon, if you find yourself a job or enrol on a training course then you can leave early, but come back in for your exams." I had a desire to help people and this was influenced by my faith, so I enrolled on a college nursing course for 2 years, but it was not commencing until May 1990. I went looking for a job that day. It was a Friday, I remember it like yesterday. It was raining very heavily. I will never forget it. I was so determined not to have to go back to school, a place I just did not want to be. I found a temporary job and thanks be to Almighty God for it. I started working as a labourer in a cash and carry that sold products to local shops and businesses. I was able to have enough spending money and give my parents something towards my living expenses. My work in the cash and carry was not easy. It was not only heavy work, staff members would make fun out of me when I was asked what I would be doing over the weekend and I would say I will be going to church. There are those who would oppose my faith, and say "Why do you believe in all that rubbish?" People used Jesus' name as blasphemy in front of me. I was new out of school and naïve so rightfully or wrongfully just accepted that having the mickey taken out of me was part of growing up in the adult world of employment. Some people are horrible.

I suppose this is the case for most young people when they leave school, which in my opinion does no good whatsoever. The old biblical quotation "An eye for an eye," came to mind. An eye for an eye leaves everyone blind I was once told (a quote from Gandhi I think). If only the people in the world heeded this. The adults I worked with said when they were younger and started work they had the Mick taken out of them so it was no different for me and that "I would get over it!" Today, that would be seen as religious discrimination, bullying and unacceptable, and thanks be to Almighty God there is now Government legislation protecting workers from this sort of treatment nowadays. I knew that I only had a few of months to put up with it before I was to enrol on my nursing course. I did enjoy helping with customer enquiries in my work, and of course having money in my pocket was nice.

I prayed throughout my time at the cash and carry for Almighty God to help me endure the everyday attack on my faith that I encountered even from senior staff. I went back in school for my exams as I promised to do. I did my best, but I had no expectation for what I was required to do or if I would do well. I passed them thank God. In May 1990, I enrolled on my City and Guilds nursing course, but before I left the cash and carry, I was told it was going into administration and would soon close down. I thank Almighty God for the personal great escape and from the mockery, and prayed for the others as this was my duty to do so. We do not have to like everyone but we are commanded to love everyone, even those who mock us. After that, I went on to work for a few weeks in a foam factory as a labourer, not exciting but earning some money all the same. It was too noisy to hear others so even if my faith was to be attacked again, I could not hear.

In November 1990, I also joined St. John Ambulance as a volunteer in the Chadderton Division. Chadderton is in Oldham. I became an Officer of the Division in 1996, and with God's help I achieved the qualification of Ambulance Aid level 2.

My work was mostly ambulance related. I found this work was very blessed by Almighty God and it would last for 8 years. The highlight of my career in St. John was doing a charity swim across Hollingworth Lake in Rochdale raising money for divisional funds, and of course going on public duty at Oldham Athletic FC and Manchester United, and at the arena in Manchester. We were often very busy though on public duty dealing with anything from a person having a nose bleed to a heart attack. But there were some perks like watching a little football or seeing some of a concert which was nice. I remember on one occasion whilst at Boundary Park (Oldham Athletic ground), I was on stretcher duty for the players. We wore bright yellow overalls and if you were on stretcher duty you were nicknamed the "Bananarama gang, "after the 1980's pop band. I was sat right in front of the Grimsby manager on one occasion, and was nearly deafened by his commands to his players! Happy times they were, but it was often so cold at Boundary Park. I am surprised those working on the ambulances did not become casualties from hypothermia!

In the November of 1990 was also a sad time for me, I was approaching age 17 when my Dad's dad, Grandad Walker passed away. I was very close to him, and he often made me laugh. I miss him. RIP Grandad x.

The full time nursing course I enrol on was for 2 years, 5 days per week with 1 day release for college study. The course consisted of practical and written assignments. I enjoyed the course. The work was very challenging and at times upsetting. Very early on in the course, I was told by a female superior that: "It is not the job for a man; it is a woman's world this, you should do something else." It was not the sort of encouragement a young person needed to be honest, but the matron instructed me to ignore such comments having overheard the comments. On one occasion my female colleagues thought it would be a great amusement to lock me in the bedroom with a patient that had just died in bed. Little did my colleagues know is that I was not afraid of the dead, but it was a little uncomfortable at first before a colleague and me started dressing the deceased to look nice for his family visiting. I remember once being told that: "It is the living you should fear, not the dead!" How right that statement was I thought. Some people loved to undermine me, their problem that. You should only look down on someone when you are helping them up. Almighty God sees everything.

With the help of my matron, my college tutor, and of course Almighty God, I successfully passed the course and the exam paper in May 1992 receiving my City and Guilds qualifications. I would continue to work in the nursing profession for the next 10 years, (1990-2000). I know why Almighty God had put me in this profession. I could development many skills and show care and compassion. I know Almighty God's gentleness came through me to the sick and the elderly. I worked for the NHS on various wards, including those suffering from mental health issues, with children, with the elderly, and with those with autism. I also worked in the community. This was hard work, but I have some fond and funny memories. One lady, I will call Mrs A was a right character. She insisted on having all the windows closed in her flat and would light a smoke as soon as I arrived. She would urinate in the bed for me to change whilst I was there instead of using her commode that she could use. Mrs A would ask me to take her out to the shops in her wheel chair. She wanted to take an adapted taxi going downhill into town, but insisted I push her up the hill back to her flat, not the other way round! I once suggested we take a taxi back up the hill, but Mrs A said: "The exercise will do you good!" One of my duties was to take her soiled laundry to the launderette. Mrs A insisted I only use half of a cup of her washing power despite me stating that in order to properly clean her soiled laundry I would require at least a full cup. Yes, her laundry came back still stained! I could write another book about all the different experiences I had over ten years in the profession!

It was soon after on 28th June 1992 that I had my second encounter with the supernatural. It was morning and I was lay in bed. I was fully awake, but decided to close my eyes again. As I did, my body began to shake like electricity was running through my body, my eyes remained closed. I had a vision, but with my eyes closed. A male figure dressed in white with bright lights behind him came closer to me from a height. I was still shaking that I had no control of and no fear. The male reached his hand out to me and offered a handshake. I did not see his face and I do not know who the person was as nothing was said between us. This was defiantly supernatural. I do not know who this was, it could have been the Lord Jesus or my grandad Walker. I am to this day not sure, but whoever it was came to me in spiritual form. It was a supernatural experience. I am 100% sure it was not a dream. I can hear the "Oh yes?" from the sceptics out there, but it is 100% true what I tell you.

I met a girl in 1992, through working voluntary on the ambulances, but the relationship did not last long because her family could accept my faith or me going to church and would often ask me: "Why are you going there?" Her mam seemed to want to argue with me. I was better off out of it. I was.

My uncle Ken (my mam's sister's husband) was tragically run over and killed in Middleton, Manchester whilst out jogging in February 1992. This was hard to understand, but accidents happen. We are in a fallen world and have no claim on Almighty God.

It was also in 1992 that whilst in the living room at home watching TV, my dad was reading the evening newspaper when he said: "They are looking for helpers at the Alexian Brothers Care Centre in Moston." I looked at the paper and became interested. I decided to give them a call as I knew the experience would be beneficial to my career. I gave the Brothers a call, and was invited by the Superior Rev Brother to attend the Centre. I was interviewed and given a role within the Care Centre by the Brother Superior and the Centre Manager. I worked at the Brothers around my hours working at the hospital. My duties would include providing personal care to retired and sick clergy – priests and religious, and people from the community that went to live in the residential part of the centre, people that had become unable to be cared for or care for themselves in their own homes.

The Alexian Brothers, a Catholic religious community dates back to the 13th century. St. Alexis was a man that dedicated his life to serving Almighty God in looking after and ministering to the sick and needy. I made a great many friends at the care home. There was Rev Fr Maurice Gordon, a Salesian priest; and in particular with the Rev Brother Bartholomew, an Alexian Brother. Everyone affectionately called him "Barty."

Barty had been in the Alexian Brothers' order for many years since he was a teenager in Ireland before coming to Manchester and working as a cook. He had been a great cook in the order for many years. When I was there, the head chef would often come up to Barty's room and ask for his opinions on cooking something or on recipes etc. Brother Bart, although retired when I met him in 1992, was obviously held in high esteem especially for his cooking ability. Barty was very well respected. Barty would tell me stories about our Lord Jesus and Mother Mary, and about the history of the Catholic faith. This I discovered was slightly different from the way I practised my Christianity, and that something was missing from my spirituality. Barty informed me that since the Last Supper of the Lord Jesus with His disciples over 2,000 years ago, this giving and receiving of Jesus' actual precious body and blood directly from heaven had been carried out ever since His crucifixion, through Apostolic succession in the Catholic church; and would continue at Holy Mass until the Lord Jesus' second coming. What a unique way Almighty God comes to us and stays with us. I recalled reading the Holy Bible when Jesus said:

"Anyone who eats my flesh and drinks my blood remains in me, and I in him."(John 6:56) I was aware of the symbolic communion service at Emmanuel Parish Church, but I thought that, if only I could have this actual body and blood of the Lord Jesus in my life, would it not bring me closer to Him? Of course it would. I learned the Lord Jesus does not only come to us in word but in sacrament. It was on the evening of Holy Thursday that Mass was born in the Upper Room. Maundy Thursday is the birthday of the Holy Mass, the Last Supper. I would be receiving the risen glorious Jesus from heaven. What an honour.

There was another person at the Alexian Brothers that looked after general maintenance of the centre, his name was Albert Jessop. In 1992, when I was on duty it was during my meal break in the canteen, Albert would often be on his break too and sit at my table. Albert would often talk to me about his experiences when he was a Franciscan Brother from 1959, and about God's love in His Divine Mercy, and the lives of the saints (in particular St Francis of Assisi and St. Faustina). Albert decided to leave the Friars in 1974. He came to the Alexian Brothers in 1976 and lived there. Albert went to a dance and met Margaret. Albert and Margaret married in 1983. Margaret also worked at the Alexian Brothers in the laundry. Albert and his wife Margaret taught me a lot about Christianity including how to pray the Chaplet of the Divine

Mercy and meditate of the mysteries of the Holy Rosary. I had never prayed in a meditation form before or given much regard to the importance of Jesus' mother. I learned that we should always pray as we can, and not as we cannot! At times, praying can be difficult so perseverance is necessary.

I was very inspired to learn that with the Lord Jesus, Mary is at the centre of God the Father's plan of salvation for us all. There are so many today that say they love the Lord Jesus, yet ignore His mother, this does not please our Lord. There seems to be a lot of confusion in the world with Mary's role and importance so let us look at this now.

When Jesus was on the cross, and saw His mother He said "**Woman, here is your son**," and to the disciple, "**Here is your mother**." From that time on, the disciple received her. (John 19:26-27). The unification took place at the words of the Lord Jesus here. All followers of the Lord Jesus (especially non-Catholics) are required to accept Mary more into their lives and homes, and not just remember Mary giving birth to Jesus. Mary was chosen before all time to be the Mother of our Lord. The Lord Jesus is God-Man; (as you will read later) this makes Mary the Mother of God. Mary is very important; we must have a special regard for her and a place for her in our hearts. This pleases Jesus. Mary is our Mother. He performed His first miracle at her request. Mary is not God nor is Mary worshipped as many non-Catholics believe she is. Mary was preserved from original sin, but was human and could have sinned because Mary had free will like we all have. We should always ask ourselves: would God, where nothing is impossible, permit His own sinless son to be born of a sinful woman? The simple answer is: No. We must be very mindful that Mary in her maternal role had an unblemished faith and she leads us more fully to her son as she did with the first apostles, supporting them when they built up the Catholic (universal) and Apostolic Church that the Lord Jesus had founded.

Our Blessed Lady, Mary, Queen of Heaven, help of Christians, often appears in different parts of the world with messages of encouragement and warnings to sinful mankind (if you did not already know). One of the most urgent messages is for mankind to turn to her son our Lord Jesus Christ in faith and accept His Divine Mercy. The other urgent message for the world to stop sinning against Almighty God, in particular her constant pleas for precious unborn babies created in the image of God not to be aborted (killed) in the womb. The most important people to Jesus are His mother and foster father, St. Joseph; and both were specially chosen by His Almighty Father God.

I am instructed by the Holy Spirit to inform you, the reader, to never be afraid to request their help to

bring you closer to the Lord Jesus and they will
support you, they work for Jesus and are with Him.
Jesus in turn brings us closer to His and Our
Father. He is our only meditator. (1 Timothy 2:5).

Saint Padre Pio 1887-1968

My good friends Albert and Margaret also taught
me about Padre Pio.

Padre Pio was a Franciscan friar who was famous
for bearing the stigmata (wounds of Jesus). I
became a spiritual child of his. He is a patron of

mine. Dear reader, never hesitate to ask St. Pio to support you and bring you closer to Jesus.

The Padre is doing a very special ministry in heaven for Almighty God. Do find out more about St. Pio's life. There are many great stories associated with him. Once, a woman came to St. Pio very troubled because her son had committed suicide. She was very concerned her son may have lost his soul. St. Pio said to her: "Do not worry, your son begged Almighty God for His mercy before he died, your son is not lost."

St. Pio once said: "I can do much more for my spiritual children in heaven than I can on earth." St. Pio certainly did that for me as I will share with you shortly. St. Pio was made a Saint by Pope John Paul II on 16th June 2002. St. Pio, pray to Jesus for us and bring us closer to Him.

The Pearl of York

St. Margaret Clithrow (1556-1586)

St. Margaret Clithrow is the patron Saint of converts (among other things). She was martyred in York by means of being crushed to death in 1586 for her faith. St. Margaret Clithrow is another patron of mine. I was very honoured to visit her shrine in York in May 2013 with my family.

St. Margaret Clithrow, pray to Jesus for us.

I learned more and more about the origins of my faith, and that the Lord Jesus had built His church on the chair of Peter (Matthew 16:17-18). St. Peter was the first Pope. I also discovered that a few had broken away to form their own churches, but this was not going to deter me wanting to be in the true fold. I started to realise that Jesus did not start His church upon Lambeth Palace or the Queen of England, but upon the Rock (St. Peter himself). Jesus said He was giving the keys to the kingdom of heaven to St. Peter.

I started attending Holy Mass in the Alexian Brothers Care Centre and I attended St. Clare's in Blackley. St. Clare's was the nearest Franciscan parish to our house. Albert had taught me about the life of St. Francis of Assisi and St. Clare and how they had given up their material lives to be poor and serve the poor. I felt very inspired by this. Little did I know, I would do the same and give up everything.

None of the saints are without sin, but by their faith and heroic lives, give us inspiration to live likewise in service for the Lord Jesus. All those who accept the Lord Jesus are Christians, and accepted by Him.

In 1993, I started attending a monthly healing mass with Albert and Margaret at St Augustine's Catholic Church in the centre of Manchester. There were so many people in attendance, and each meeting lasted for 3/4 hours. There was lively worship, laying on of hands, confessions, and holy mass. Each person would queue up, say their intention privately and be prayed over. I had mentioned on a few occasions in the prayer group about my bad headaches. The lay man that ran the prayer group with his wife said "You must pray more and a lot about this!" I did ask the Lord Jesus to heal me, and I requested the help and support of Our Blessed Lady, mindful that Jesus' first miracle was at her request. St. Padre Pio was also speaking to Jesus about it. A short time after that meeting, I had a dream. My dream was this, I was in bed asleep and St. Padre Pio came to the top of my bed (despite the top of my bed being against the wall,) he was dressed in his Franciscan religious habit with his hood up. He placed both hands on the top of my head. He was wearing his mittens as he often did to cover his stigmatized hands. He never said anything, but when I woke up I remembered what had happened very clearly. I knew that this was a sign that my prayers had been heard and something would be done about my bad headaches.

In December of 1993, whilst at Christmas party in Oldham organised by St John Ambulance, I was waiting outside the premises at the end of the evening for a lift home. I was set upon by three men for no reason. I was caught completely unaware (not good practice for a martial artist, is it?!). I did sustain some injuries and I needed hospital treatment, but thanks be to Almighty God I had no broken bones or permanent injuries. The Rev Fr who was the Chaplain at the Royal Oldham Hospital at the time who knew me was on his rounds. I remember Fr saying to me at the time: "Simon, some people just behave like animals." The three men (all brothers) were arrested by the police nearby. I learned a very valuable lesson that night never to let anyone too close to my personal space, and I not to be naïve especially with strangers. I also learned that people do not need a motive to do evil. Spiritually I was left feeling quite bitter towards my attackers for a while, and prayed for God's help to forgive them. Through months of reflection about this, I became aware that the devil himself had used these three men to get rid of me and try and end my life.

The year 1994 was a busy year. In the April of it was the beginning of a three day trial. I gave my evidence as did the other witnesses including the police. My family and I were in court for two days. I was the first witness. I gave my account despite being nervous, but when I was cross examined the defence solicitor did her best to portray me as a trouble maker and a liar. I could see the devil working in her. All she was interested in was getting her lads off the hook and her pay cheque, I thought. With Almighty God's help, I stayed focused and did not make eye contact, looking only at the judges. We were not required on the third day for the sentencing. I was informed via telephone that all three brothers were sent to jail. Without Almighty God's help, I would not have been able to forgive my attackers, but thanks to Him I have been able to since the attack on my life. If Almighty God is willing to forgive me of all my sins, I must forgive my trespassers whoever they are; and yes, even those that tried to kill me! This was evil again at work, but Almighty God would not let evil prevail.

After my recovery, I obtained some additional part time work with social services working as a Day Centre Support Worker. I juggled this work with my hospital work and my service at the Alexian Brothers Care Centre. All I ever did was work, a bit of a workaholic you might say. I enjoyed working at the day centre looking after older people. There was not as much hands on nursing as at the hospital. I led activities to keep the clients aka service users, occupied between them having their lunch and a chat with each other. Many of the clients were retired or used the centre to give their carer/spouse a rest. I would bake scones and call the numbers out for bingo. My service at the centre would last 3 years. In my last year I discovered that there were an additional 12 and half hours up for grabs, but I would need to apply internally. I willingly did, and if successful I would resign from the hospital. I was tipped off however by a male colleague that my superiors' best friend was applying for a transfer and he said: "She will get the job Simon; they are all the best of buddies." I took on board what he said and would bear his comments in mind. I had my interview, and because I was already doing the job and I knew all the service users. I answered the questions precisely without any hesitations. After my interview I went straight out the office and started calling out the numbers for bingo. Soon after, the lady in question to be interviewed came in the building full of smiles, and was greeted by my superiors' in a very over welcoming manner. There certainly did not seem to be any nerves. I could see from where I was sat calling out the numbers, the office where the interview was taking place. I saw loads of laughing and all three were enjoying a cup of something. Well, my male colleague was bang on. She was offered the position. My male colleague, when I told him said: "I told you, but it is not right this hand picking of people Simon." But what could I do? I just continued working between the hospital and the day centre. I trusted Almighty God was watching.

Almighty God continued His work and it was in 1994, whilst at the monthly meeting prayer group in St Augustine's, Manchester, my life was about to change forever. It was at the end of the prayer meeting, and I was about to leave when a man walked towards the pew where I was sat, and said:

"We know you need some prayers so please come to the back and we will pray over you." I said: "You are right, I do, and I keep having bad headaches and I have put up with it for many of years." The man replied: "We know." I walked to the back of the church with the man, and a group of five people 3 men and 2 ladies, laid their hands on me and started to pray and give thanks to the Lord Jesus. I was very shocked to be informed by one member of the group that my long history of bad headaches was being caused by Almighty God's enemy and the terrible enemy of mankind, the devil himself. The devil had assigned a demon to cause me great discomfort, tiredness, and distraction, not only in life, but also, in my walk with the Lord Jesus. In the Lord Jesus Christ's name, the pain, and the demon left my head at once, and I felt as light as a feather! I was full of mixed emotions, full of tears of joy. I had no pain and felt very at ease. The lady said: "Do not worry Simon, the pain the devil had given you that supernatural attack, will never come back. It has been sent back to hell by the power of the Lord Jesus!"

I recall the help St. Padre Pio's gave me when he came to me in the dream in 1992. In my dream, I saw him come to the top of my bed dressed in his religious habit with his hood up and mittens on to cover the piercing on his hands. St. Padre Pio said nothing to me, but placed his hands on my head. Little was I to know through his intercession and help was I to be healed from the pain in my head and to this day the pain never returned. I had so many helpers from heaven giving glory and praise to the Lord Jesus.

I also recalled what it said in the Bible about **every knee bowing at the name of Jesus** (Philippians 2:10). The lady at St Augustine's went on to tell me that Jesus is so powerful against the devil. Her example was for me to compare myself to a little spider that I could put my foot on at any time! No wonder the tablets the doctor gave me would not work I thought, this was a spiritual attack! The lady went on to tell me that I was to put on the full armour of Almighty God Himself (Ephesians 6:11) and work for Almighty God's glory. I never got the names of those Almighty God used to heal me, and I have never seen or spoken to them since to this day. I know that what happened that day was real and was a miracle from Almighty God Himself, and He used those people who loved Him to answer my prayers and heal me. I decided after some reflection that I would start attending the local Catholic Church every Sunday. The people at Emmanuel Parish Church were very understanding as I could not attend both parishes because the service times were the same. In later years, I discovered that the church hall at Emmanuel had been burnt down, and a block of flats were built. I was very saddened to hear this. I have fond memories spending time in fellowship with other

Christians in that church hall. We all love the same Lord Jesus despite Theological differences. I do not know if the fire was started deliberately or not, but it is a shame the hall is no more. Anyway, I would start attending Corpus Christi (which means Body of Christ) Catholic Church, Hollinwood. Corpus Christi was the nearest Catholic parish to our house in Chadderton even though it is in Hollinwood. The parish priest was the Rev Fr Rawson. I recall the first time I introduced myself to Fr Rawson in 1996. He was very witty and funny, yet I would describe him as a very holy and devout man.

I would always go up for a spiritual blessing which ever Catholic Church I was in. This blessing was very meaningful to me even though I was not yet in full communion with the Catholic Church. My feelings for Almighty God were getting stronger and stronger, and no doubt people thought I was going too far with this journey. Some must have thought I was brainwashed! I have reflected about this over the years. To have a devotion to Almighty God is seen as odd, but not to plaster posters of a pop band over the bedroom walls or never stop talking about a favourite football team in this world. But if you love Almighty God, some people think you are crazy. If you inform most people that you are going to church, they raise their eyebrows. This was my experience with people anyway, but my family, although did not attend church, were supportive. I just wanted Almighty God's will for me, and this has not changed. I simply believed, although I did not understand it all, that Almighty God loved me. Almighty God loves everyone, but people do not believe it or do not want to be involved.

I was a regular visitor at St Clare's Friary during 1996, and Albert knew the Guardian there, a Rev Fr Aidan OFM Conv. They were young novices back in the early 1960's in the Franciscan college. On one occasion when I was leaving, I could not get my car to start outside the friary. Fr Aidan had just blessed my car. I was stuck and stranded so I called my dad. My dad said he did not have any jump leads so would contact my Grandad Beddow (his father in law). My grandad was not a believer and was a straight talker. He would say what he thought. When my dad and grandad arrived outside the friary, Rev Fr Aidan was still standing with me. My grandad said: "Where is Jesus then to help you?" I felt a little embarrassed and did not know what to say in reply. My dad calmly said: "He has brought you here to help us!" Well, just how right my dad was. My grandad remained silent and we got my little car going again.

In 1997, my Nana Beddow passed away. This knocked us for six in particular my mam. Nana Beddow was a lovely lady and deeply spiritual. Nana had suffered from strokes but never complained. She loved our Lord Jesus very much, and no doubt enjoying heaven now. RIP Nana Beddow, I miss you. x

I decided after 5 years of discernment that I wanted to become a full member of the Catholic Church and I would have the same entitlements as other Catholics, most importantly being able to receive and worship the precious body and blood of Christ Himself into my body and soul and all the other sacraments. It is such a unique way that Our Lord comes to us and gives us focus. I also got in contact with the Franciscan Friars in London, and corresponded with them, yet left my options open as to where Almighty God wanted me. I expressed an interest in undertaking a study programme within the Church known as Rite of Christian Initiation of Adults (RCIA). I would attend Corpus Christi every week as well as on Sunday for my instruction on the Faith. Within a few months, I was received into the Catholic Church at St Clare's, Blackley on 23rd September 1997. Albert and Margaret became my Godparents. It was only weeks after the deaths of Princess Diana and Mother Teresa (now St. Teresa). I was not aware until sometime later that the 23rd September was the date when St. Padre Pio had died in 1968. I thought that was ironic as the date was chosen for me by the Rev Fr Aidan who did not know my love for the Padre.

The Church was full at my reception in St. Clare's, mostly full of people I did not know, but all wished me the best for my future in faith. The service was not a posh or grand one, but simple. My friend Barty was not well enough to attend unfortunately, however he was delighted for me, and to see Barty happy made me happy. Barty's health had taken a turn for the worse and he died soon after on 9th December 1997, aged 82. It was a sad time for me, but I was happy that he was with Almighty God in heaven and I knew he was happy I had become a Catholic, something I know he was praying and hoping for. I was also fortunate enough to be able to attend his funeral although it was difficult to change my shifts. On the day of Barty's funeral, I was working the late shift so could attend in the morning without any problems. I thought how Almighty God must plan these things! Barty's family came over from Ireland too. The Chaplain at the Alexian Brothers at that time was the Rev Fr Timothy, a lovely, well-spoken priest. He gave Barty a good send off!

In 1997, I applied for a job at The National Autistic Society and thanks be to Almighty God I was successful. I left work at the hospital and the day centre and started work in Manchester as an Adult Support Worker. This was a hard job, but was very rewarding looking after young adults with autism. I worked there for three years whilst strongly considering a religious vocation.

Back In 1998, I felt it was the right time to get my own place and become more independent. I think at first my parents were a bit saddened by this thinking that they had done something wrong to me. I assured them they had not! I had just got to that stage in my life to fly the nest as some would say.

I saw in the newspaper a maisonette for sale in Chadderton, not far from my parents, and I had saved just enough money. My dad kindly let me borrow some money to furnish the place. I moved in, and moved parishes to St. Herbert's. The Rev Fr Mckie was the Parish Priest. I resigned from St. John Ambulance after 8 years' service, and started voluntary work as a Home Watch Coordinator working with the local police. This was very interesting work, and I had a great deal of personal reward helping and looking out for residents that lived near me especially those that were elderly. I also enjoyed my fair share of drinking tea in group meetings.

Within a short time of having my own space, I was able to meditate more and learn more about Almighty God. I started taking Biblical correspondence courses with the Emmaus Bible School UK and The Salvation Army. I would greatly recommend anyone wishing to learn more about Almighty God's word – The Holy Bible, to undertake some courses. The tutors are very supportive and encouraging.

I was a regular visitor at my parents' house, whilst having and enjoying my own independence. I also went on spiritual retreats that were very uplifting. I just loved the space to be on my own with Almighty God. It was while I was on retreat that an urgent message had been left for me and I was asked by the Rev Fr there to phone home urgently. In a state of spiritual bliss, I wondered what could be wrong. I phoned home, and my mother said: "Margaret your Godmother has phoned up, and she was crying, Albert has been told by the doctor he has deadly cancer in his throat, and would you all pray for him?" I was in shock, and said "Of course." We entrusted Albert to Almighty God's care. Here is Albert's story in his own words from his book: Miracles Often Happen, witness to the Divine Mercy 2008. (Permission granted). Albert's writes:

It was during February 1998, and six months before my retirement from work that I had a very frightening dream. In my dream, I was walking down the right hand side of the road and coming towards me on the left side, I saw Satan (the devil) consuming a soul feet first. Satan saw me and said: "I will get you in three months' time." When morning came I told my wife Margaret. She said: "Everyone has dreams of some kind," and that was that. But the dream stayed with me for some time.

Three months to the day, I began to notice a swelling on the left side of my neck. I went to see my doctor who told me I had swollen glands, and gave me some pills. After some time, there was no improvement in the swelling, and it got very much worse. It was time to change my doctor and get a second opinion. I was told that I had lymphomas, which is the second biggest cancer killer after lung cancer. Well, things began to happen, and I was rushed into the North Manchester General Hospital. After an examination, I was told that I had to have an operation on the Monday after. I then started to have difficulty with my breathing, and it was not until I asked Our Blessed Lady to help me that I was able to breathe freely. The doctors decided to operate right away. It was on the operating table that I began my encounter with the Lord. I could see very black smoke all around me and I knew it was from hell. I had no fear since I had placed my will in the Lord's hands. Then I saw this very bright circle of light keeping back the black smoke. It was then that I heard the voice of the Lord:

"**The bright light is the prayers being offered for your soul**." Albert then saw the Lord Jesus on the cross, and the Lord Jesus said: "**Your suffering and mine are for the salvation of sinners in the world today, since few are willing to suffer for them**." Albert continues; next Jesus showed me pictures of where I was at fault in my life. He placed before me the words Horse racing, Lotto, and fruit machines. Through my weakness for gambling, much money had been wasted. He pulled all these

images together and said: "**It's a fool's game.**"
Then He showed me two hearts divided by a wedge
of gambling: "**Take away this wedge, and your
heart and mine will become one.**" Jesus then
went on to remind me of a dream I had about a
horse called "Example," ridden by Lester Piggott,
which won the next day for me at a price of 11-2.
He said: "**I want you to place at the top of your
priorities the word "Example." You have
reached the peak of the mountain, and now you
are coming down the other side.**" He was
referring to my age. Jesus added: "**When you were
a child, you were spotless in my sight. Now you
are to return to be the child you once were, and
I myself will take you to heaven in my arms.
Remember the banner you made of my Divine
Mercy? You are to complete it and you are to
have it blessed by your parish priest.**" Then
because I was thinking that he might not agree to
bless the banner; Jesus said directly:

"**Your Reverend Father Seale.**" "**All who spread
this devotion will encounter many great
blessing in their lives and many evils will
disappear. Many miracles will take place
through the banner, and everyone who has a
picture of the Divine Mercy in their home, or on
their person, will always have my care. I want
you to shout my name from the rooftops,
because there is little time left before my
second coming.**"

The seal of approval for Albert's work came at a time when Albert was receiving treatment in hospital, and wondering whether his encounters with the Lord Jesus was all in his mind. One day, Albert was sat in his chair near his bed. Albert reported that as he looked at the Divine Mercy image of Jesus in his book, he said this quiet prayer: "Dear Jesus, when I smile at anyone, will you smile through me?" Just then the consultant came on the ward doing his rounds, he came to Albert's bed, and the first thing he said to Albert was: "Mr Jessop, how is it you always give me a beautiful smile?" Albert had other encounters with the Lord Jesus that you can read for yourself in his book Miracles Often Happen, witness to the Divine Mercy published in 2008. The Divine Mercy Prayer Group in Moston started in 1998 in the Alexian Brothers Care Centre.

In 1999, I had begun discerning more seriously whether I had a vocation as a priest or religious.

One day in 1999 whilst visiting my parents, there was a knock at the door. It was my old friend from school Mark who had moved away. He was back and living in Manchester, was getting married and wanted to invite me. It was great to see him again, and of course I attended.

I started to consider serving Almighty God in full time ministry. I was fully aware that although since

1990 I had learnt more and achieved more than I did at school, I was probably not educated enough to become a priest or a religious. This was something I prayed about very hard if this was Almighty God's will for me. I was reminded in Holy Scripture what Our Lord said:

"Whoever wants to be my disciple must deny themselves, take up their cross, and follow me." (Luke 9:23). I decided to pursue a vocation. I visited the Friars in person and applied to a seminary college in London run by the Society of Jesus (Jesuits). The college was called Campion House. I was interviewed by the Principal, the Rev Fr Michael Barrow SJ.

The work of Campion House started in 1919, and was well known in England for assisting men and those working in ministry, yet especially for those that had not done very well at school for whatever reason (this was me!)   Campion House was named after St. Edmund Campion SJ, a priest and martyr.

St. Edmund Campion was martyred in London for the faith in 1581. St Edmund Campion is another patron of mine. St. Edmund Campion, pray to Jesus for us. St. Edmund Campion is one of the forty martyrs of England and Wales. All were executed between 1535 -1679. They were canonized (made saints) by Pope Paul VI on 25th October 1970. The forty martyrs of England and Wales pray to Jesus for us.

The Saints are constantly helping us and supporting us by their prayers. Each Saint is given a special job to do from heaven. There is not just St. Christopher helping travellers. Each Saint has his/her work to do for Almighty God. What a great honour working for our Creator in heaven.

Anyway, by the turn of the millennium, I felt Almighty God was directing in my life towards full ministry, and after some careful thought, I decided to put my house up for sale. I gave up my job and gave my car to my brother Trevor. Trevor was in the army, and he needed a car for coming home at weekends and when he was on leave. Did I have any need for material things I would often remind myself? The Lord Jesus told me in His word that: **"You can't serve two masters, God and money."** (Matthew 6:24). I prayed my house would sell quickly as I was preparing myself for full time ministry. It was not long before I was due to leave for London that a young man came to view my house, and said he was interested but was on low wages. I knew that Almighty God was testing me at that point, and if I would be charitable? Anyway, I dropped the price, and said: "I will leave everything in for you as well." This was definitely by Almighty God's grace that I did this, no credit to me. The young man was obviously very happy. I was as well because I had no obstacles in my way. The Friars in London and staff at Campion House advised me to be realistic and not completely separate myself from material things as I had a desire to do; but to put the money away in case things did not work out for me as a student. I took their wise counsel and did this. Almighty God will provide I thought. I just need to continue trusting Him. The process for being accepted into training was not a quick one and I was required to undergo a total of nine interviews over a weekend with different people in the seminary including members of the Jesuit community, religious sisters and the college principal. Thanks to Almighty God, I passed and was accepted.

My first day at Campion House was of course quite a nervous one with attending inductions etc. There were ten of us training for the priesthood, including myself. We were all there for the same purpose: to serve Almighty God and our neighbours. One man had come all the way from Vietnam to serve. There was another man David from Scotland. He was a reformed character. I remember being out with Dave in London on one occasion when Dave had a violent convulsion. Dave believed the devil personally attacked him and caused him to suffer. Dave shouted out "Heavenly Father." Dave said he had never had any health problems previously, and after the event he went for tests at Hounslow hospital and he was given the all clear. Nothing was found wrong with his health.

Life in community at Campion House did take some getting used to. I had come from living on my own to living with a group of other men. We all shared facilities, but had our own small room. Although small, it was cosy with my own sink and radiator. The staff could not do enough for us, and we would always get nice meals from the chef and the housekeepers always ensured we had clean bedding every week. The subjects we studied were: English language, spoken English, Spirituality, Human Development, Sacred Liturgy, Sacristan training, Latin, Pastoral training, Philosophy, Parish placement, and of course we studied Theology. We would say the Divine office of the church at prayer times, and have holy mass every day. Within the first week, my weaknesses certainly became very clear to my superiors. The Jesuits have a gift and a speciality for discerning. It was noted that when it was my turn to read at mass (that I dreaded with butterflies in my stomach), I was not pronouncing my H's! I was informed that this could be a northern England habit from those living in the south of England. The Rev Superior, Fr. Nye SJ would spend time with me at reading lessons. I found it difficult to read as my mind would race faster than I could get the words out, and even though my eyesight was okay, I struggled reading the words. It seemed fuzzy to me. I will tell you how Almighty

God in His goodness answered my prayers to that later.

In my spoken English class, my teacher noticed that when I was reading, I was saying words that were not in the text. He wanted me to be assessed and said the college would arrange for a Clinical Psychologist to come in and give me some educational tests. This happened and my brain was grilled by him for two hours. His findings found that I did have a mild form of dyslexia. I was so grateful that this had been found out, and that I could learn new methods of learning and receive extra time in exams. But I was saddened that I went through all those years at school and no one detected anything. I had been seen as just another kid that could not be bothered, I think!

As a result of the specialist's findings, I was advised to drop the Latin class, which I was not too bothered about because Latin would have only been said by me after ordination, and if I was to say a Latin mass. It lifted a great weight off my shoulders! I could concentrate on the other subjects, as my timetable was a busy one. I was not the only one to have a learning difficulty. It was just that the other students already knew what kind of help they needed when they came to Campion House. I received support from a tutor that came in college every week that helped me immensely. I learned new educational skills and brushed up on what was lacking. It was very hard work, but who said working for Almighty God would be easy? I would remind myself of this.

The human development classes were very interesting, and we were joined by lay ministry students that worked in different parishes, and some religious sisters. As a class, each week we would look into a topic and what effects the topic would have on each of us, i.e. conflict resolution, dealing with authority etc. We had fun as well. I really learned a lot about myself, and others. I am grateful to Margaret, our tutor, for all her support in human development.

Each student had their own individual Counsellor appointed by the college. There was another lady called Margaret who was my Counsellor. She was based in Kilburn, North West London. It was a nice time for me and each student to get out of college for the afternoon, see our counsellor for the hour, then go sightseeing around London or just take time out. At times, the counselling sessions were hard going though, especially if life in the community was not running smoothly. There were also times when things needed getting off my chest to Margaret, and she was a great help to me. The devil was forever trying to disturb the peace in the community at Campion House, and we knew he did not like all those prayers and worship to Almighty

God. We were all given a Spiritual Director to consult as well, and this was most useful too.

At the start of each term, each student was given specific roles within the college. Every student would have a go at each task. One of the tasks was Student Coordinator/Guardian. This was not easy, and at times you would need to be a sounding board and a referee between the students when there was any conflict. It was with the guidance of the Holy Spirit that everything was resolved, and thanks be to Almighty God there was nothing serious that needed sorting out. But like with any workplace, there were clashes of personalities.

I was very honoured to work in the Sacristy, and set up things for Holy mass. Whilst there, I would often think that what I was a part of, had been going on for over 2,000 years! I was mindful that I was in a holy place because the Lord Jesus was a part of the place! Each student was also put on a parish placement every Sunday. I was placed in a parish in Brentford under the guidance of the Rev Fr Jim. He was from Scotland. He was a very funny and direct man. I was taught a lot by him, including how to serve on the altar. On one occasion, I inadvertently made Father blush whilst he was saying mass. He was at the part of the mass when peace with each other is exchanged. I was standing next to him and walked off the altar to share peace (shake hands) with the younger servers and members of the congregation in the front pews. As I walked back to my place, I kicked a bell which one of the young servers had not returned. Well, needless to say, I nearly went flying! Everyone must have seen me or at least heard the bell go off when I kicked it. I learned very quickly after that to always look where I was walking, even on Almighty God's altar!

Whilst I was in the seminary in London in 2002, my mam's aunty Sarah died, a very straight talker. RIP Aunty Sarah. x

My pastoral work was Almighty God again working in such a powerful way. I was privileged to work at Providence Row in the East End of London working in their centre that catered for people that were homeless and those living in poverty. For a first world country, let me tell you dear reader, it was disgraceful people would be living in those circumstances. One of my tasks was lifting the heavy pots for the Rev Sisters. So simple a task I would often think, yet the nuns needed me there to do it. I remember on one occasion I was emptying the dish washer and the plates were very hot, I needed to use a tea towel to empty it. As I was serving the hot broth to the people, I said to a homeless man: "Please be careful. The plate is hot." He replied: "That is okay, I am freezing. I have been out all night and it will warm me up!" This was an eye opener to me. He just took the plate and he did not even flinch or drop the hot plate as I would have done. At that time the weather was very cold. Many people would put lots of pepper on their food to warm themselves up. How lucky the people in that centre made me feel. I was learning about those much less fortunate in life all the time.

All the students at Campion House had been invited to a high Anglo Catholic service in London on one occasion, and the Archbishop of Canterbury, Dr Williams, would be in attendance. All the students were there and afterwards we were invited for refreshments. The people were all very posh and appeared well off. We were expecting a brew and a biscuit, but were offered sherry in expensive glasses. What a contrast, I thought from what I experienced at Providence Row working with those labelled as the down and outs, and dredges of society, but how wrong they were about those people. I saw Almighty God through them. It is the great divide between rich and poor I thought and in Almighty God's sight! I recall in 2002 the students and I were watching the funeral of the Queen Mother. The hearse was set to travel up the Great West road right near our college and end towards central London. A few of us stood on the pavement and returned back to college to watch the funeral on TV. We then went back out to see the hearse pass by, and back to her resting place. I am by no means a big royalist, but it was where I lived. On many another occasions, we would hear and see concord fly into Heathrow Airport around 6 miles away. Every time this happened, you could feel the building shake. What an experience that was. Most of the courses I had undertaken were attendance courses and I benefited a great deal.

The course ended at Campion House after 2 years. We all left on a sad note because we were informed that the Jesuits were to leave Campion House, and that the General Superior of the Jesuits had informed the Jesuit community including the students that Campion House was to close after many years helping people, in particular men training for the priesthood and the laity. I had taken a lot from my time at Campion House especially the life experience. I met some great people and Almighty God in His goodness gave me some great opportunities from working in worm wood scrubs to supporting those on the streets. The Lord had worked in a wonderful way. I knew more about myself and understood people's needs better, thanks to Campion House, and I became less naïve and developed well. Campion House closed in 2004 after providing assistance to students since 1919.

The next place in my formation process was at St Cuthbert's College, Ushaw in Durham. Before attending the next part of my formation, I was on a summer retreat at Cleator Moor in the Lake District, a lovely prayerful place. No wonder William

Wordsworth was so inspired surrounded by Almighty God's beauty. It was here that the Mother of God, Mary spoke to me. I was in meditation in the church, and my mind began to wander as it often does. No one said prayer was easy. I started thinking about material wealth. I asked Almighty God to make me rich and wealthy, and I asked Our Lady to give me the winning numbers for the up and coming Lotto draw on Saturday. Talk about being blunt with the Mother of God! Mother Mary very gently and beautifully spoke to my heart and said: **"Simon, that's not what it is about."** I learned from Our Lady and Blessed Mother on that day to not focus on having treasures on earth. To this day I cannot understand why I would be so cheeky and blunt with the Mother of God. It was here at St. Cuthbert's College that I spent a long time when not in lessons in quiet meditation and contemplation. I became increasingly troubled and needed to seriously discern whether the ordained ministry was for me. I did convince myself that working for Almighty God was for me, but at the same time I did this, my spirit became very restless in regards to becoming an ordained priest. I could do nothing but address my concerns publicly. I would often meet with my Spiritual Director and my Superiors, and try and make sense of why I was feeling this way. What I did find most difficult was not the staff, other students, or the studies, but being institutionalized with very little privacy. We all studied together, prayed together, ate together, and were expected to socialise together too! As a private person needing my own space, this became difficult for me without being anti-social. After a lot more prayer and discernment; it became evident to me that I was simply "**Going against the grain**" with this lifestyle. I decided to speak with my Superiors and ask for the permission to leave the formation process after a while. This was granted.

I left with my superior's blessing and with the blessings and good wishes of my peers in the seminary. I had done nothing wrong but I could not fool myself any longer, and I certainly could not fool Almighty God or pretend I was happy! I know that my formation process was God's will for me for the years I was in, and it was Almighty God's will that my formation should finish before my ordination. Almighty God had other plans for my life. I have no regrets for going in or coming out of the seminary. I received a Grade B in my Theology exam. That itself was a miracle. I left Durham and returned to Manchester.

My parents came to my rescue, and said I could move back in their home or I could have been without a place to live. I did move back in with my parents in November 2003, over five years after moving out.

With my mam and dad, Sandra and Kevin at Lyme Park, Cheshire

My mam said: "Are you sure you are okay about leaving the seminary? Does it feel like a divorce?" My mam has been married to my dad since 1971, and has never been divorced so her question was a difficult one to understand. I replied: "No mam, it is Almighty God's will. He will not abandon me. I have no regrets for trying the priesthood or leaving it. I have learnt a lot and Almighty God must have other plans for my life." Almighty God did indeed have other plans.

I returned back to my home parish of Corpus Christi, and told the Rev Fr Rawson that I had left the seminary. His reply was simply, "Well it is not for everyone. Almighty God does not love you any less Simon." I signed up to a local nursing agency and thanks to Him, quickly found work. I was aware I was no longer living rent free like in the seminary!

In May 2003, my brother Paul got married to Hayley and I was his best man. (They have two children, my nephew Kian born in 2006 and my niece Darcey born in 2011.)

Only days later after being his best man, tragically my cousin David was killed in a car accident, age 29. RIP David. Eleven years previously, his dad (my uncle) was run over and killed. RIP Uncle Ken.

After leaving the seminary at the end of 2003, I applied to the police force of Greater Manchester working in the neighbourhood policing department. I was interviewed by a Police Inspector and a panel, and thanks to Almighty God I was accepted. I was sent a letter by the Chief Superintendent. The Police Inspector stated that with my pastoral experience, I would be ideal as an officer on the Neighbourhood Policing Team as this was at the heart of what Policing is. I obviously felt very happy to be successful and honoured that people had faith in me to be an asset to the policing team. No doubt throughout the world at a job interview, if you state you are a Christian it could go against you, especially if those interviewing you are against Almighty God and/or have something against those who love Almighty God! Many people have lost their jobs, even have paid with their own lives for admitting they love Almighty God.

Anyway, I was instructed to not give up the work I was doing, as the process could take a bit of time because of the vetting processes etc. I started training at Sedgley Park in April 2004, and was to be stationed at Oldham Police Station. I would be working in Derker. I was not very happy at Sedgley Park during my Officer Safety Training (OST) though because the instructor asked if anyone did a martial art; and when I told him I did, he stated that martial arts did not work, should never be used, and only use what he was demonstrating for self-defence when on duty. How wrong he was I thought, but I could not say anything because he would have reported me to my Inspector so I just did what I was told. I needed to use Aikido on a few occasions, but never the OST. It was not great. One can defend themselves even against someone holding a gun with Aikido (thankfully I did not need to) but with OST, an officer would need to surrender and wait for armed response officers. This is the problem with bank robberies in this country.

It was in 2004 that my Grandad Beddow died. I miss him. RIP Grandad x.

My prayer while in the police was for Almighty God to walk with me, in front and behind me, for the intentions of the people of Derker where I worked, and that the known criminals in the area would not hate me because of the job I was doing. In time, my belief in the Lord Jesus was no secret to the residents of Derker, even those up to no good, and I felt that people had respect for me because of the Lord Jesus, all glory and praise to Him. In 2005, I was nominated for a Pride of Oldham award for the work I had carried out in the community I served, which was run by the local authority. I did not win the award outright, but to be recognised for my efforts was very moving for me.

I started to look for my own place again and pulled my resources together. I saw a home for sale in the newspaper, and with a driveway. It was in Manchester. Having a driveway was pretty much up there on my priority list, (it did get difficult to park when I lived at my maisonette). I arranged to speak with the estate agent and the seller. The seller's name was Mr Wood. He informed me that he had lived in the house for many years with his wife, but she had died quite recently, and it was not the same in the house without her. He said that he dreaded closing the curtains at night, and that he felt so lonely. Mr Wood said the house had been looked after, but that the only problem he had was with the next door neighbour. Mr Wood elaborated that on occasions, the neighbour would play music but that she would fell asleep with the music on, and he would have to knock on her door quite late. I thought I could handle that as I loved my fair share of music. I would often wear headphones though. Mr Wood was planning to live in Morecambe. He showed me and my parents that had come to support me and give me their views of the place around the house and as we were leaving he said: "I will tell you what Simon, I will knock 500 quid off the asking price, and I will leave everything in for you." I suddenly remembered the time when I was selling my home, and gave the young lad everything in my house because he would be starting with nothing, starting from scratch. I knew in my heart that this was Almighty God working. My heart knew He was giving me back the material items I had given away and that I now needed again - microwave, washing machine, beds, wardrobes, etc. My dad said: "It is a massive help to you Simon." It felt so right so I applied for a mortgage. I moved into my new home in August 2004. I sure knew it was Almighty God's work and helping me immensely, and was no coincidence.

I introduced myself to the parish priest the Rev Fr Denneny, Rural Dean (in charge of the deanery containing several parishes). I became a member of Christ the King Catholic Church and soon after volunteered to become a parish minibus driver on Sundays. The parish offered a free service and collected anyone having difficulty getting to church. I would pick up parishioners and ensure they get to mass and home again.

I was eager to make a difference in my area where I had moved to, and in a short time became a Community Guardian with Manchester City Council - a voluntary role in that a resident "adopts the community in which they live." The role mainly focuses on environmental issues within that community, from litter picking, to reporting a street light that was not working etc. I soon became a Community Guardian Mentor, supporting others wanting to become Community Guardians. My efforts of hard work were recognised in 2013 when I was the runner up for the Neighbour of the Year Award in Manchester.

It was during 2004, my first year in my new home that my faith was tested like never before. My neighbour that played music only on occasions started playing music more often, and it started to disturb my spirit greatly especially at night, even when I was wearing ear plugs. I prayed but things were not getting any better. My neighbour ignored my plea! The local authority got involved because I needed to report it because my quality of life (and no sleep) were being greatly affected. It was party after party with loud music and very raised voices. It was over 18 months later that on one occasion my neighbour came to my door crying because she had been reprimanded for her behaviour from the authorities. She looked at the light above my door that came on when you walk near it. She said: "We are all heading for the light," and started singing rap music swearing to me using Almighty God's name. My neighbour claimed to be a follower of the Lord Jesus too! I knew it was all a pack of lies though. My neighbour started swearing and singing at me. I thought she had taken something. It was at that time my spirit saw two snakes, one black, and one white on each of her shoulders. Both were spitting venom in my direction. Of course this was not a physical experience, but a spiritual one and the devil thought he had won. At that time, Almighty God gave me a tremendous peace though, and I was not frightened as you would expect me to be of the devil. I remember saying gently to her: "You should not treat Almighty God like that." My neighbour just ignored me and went back to her home. I was informed after a short time that she was ordered to move out of her house by the authorities. I knew something must have happened because it had gone very quiet at night and I was not being woken up like I had been. I prayed in thanksgiving to Almighty God, but at the same time wondered why I was to endure this for so long. I know Almighty God was testing me, and building up my endurance, and all the more I needed to trust Him. The Lord answered me in His word:

"Be still in the presence of the Lord (me), and wait patiently for Him (me) to act. Don't worry about evil people who prosper or fret about their wicked schemes. Stop being angry! Turn from your rage! Do not lose your temper- it only leads to harm for the wicked will be destroyed, but those who trust in the Lord (me) will possess the land." (Psalm 37:7-9).

One day whilst on duty in the police force, patrolling down Acre lane in Derker, an elderly lady came to the door, and introduced herself. Her name was Kath. I also introduced myself. Kath said "Hello are you our new bobby? If you are ever passing just knock on and I will make you a brew and give you a biscuit. We have always had a good bond on here with the local bobby!" she added. I thought that this lady has been sent by Almighty God, another offer of a cup of tea! Kath was very aware that I would be out in all weathers. How nice to be considered, I thought. The local Catholic Church was the parish of the Sacred Heart. It was difficult for me to get to 9am morning mass because when I was on the early shift, the police briefings would often last a while from coming on duty at 8.30am.

I had only known Kath for a few weeks when one morning, she informed me she had received a letter through the post stating that her home was in the red zone. The letter came from the housing market renewal team and was marked for demolition. This was part of the regeneration plans for the local area from the local authority. Kath was mortified to say the least. Kath did not have any family in England, just a daughter and relatives that lived in the Netherlands. The Derker action group was set up by residents in the red zone, and Kath became a member as I knew she would do. I would often be on duty when meetings were held between the housing authorities, counsellors and angry residents. It would get very heated to say the least. I needed to publicly remain impartial, yet I felt a deep sadness for Kath and the others that were mostly elderly, and that had been a pillar for the Derker community for many years. Kath had lived in her home for years. All the residents knew that I supported their cause, but also that I was there to serve everyone, even the people I did not politically agree with. There was nothing wrong with Kath's house or the others yet the authorities wanted to move Kath and her close friends out. Kath would often tell me: "This is my home Simon. I have fond memories living here. I do not want to go in a flat and all my friends live around here."

My friend Kath was also a devout Catholic, and we developed a close friendship. Kath appreciated me bringing bits in for her, and I appreciated a hot brew when the weather was bad, and of course her company and fellowship. Kath said on one occasion: "I am too old for all this hassle. I would rather die first than leave here." Kath trusted the Lord and had no fear, but was under a lot of stress as were the other residents. The resistance from Kath and the Derker action group became so strong that the authorities wanted to obtain a CPO (compulsory purchase order). I could see that over the weeks and months, it had taken its toll on Kath's health, but she plodded on. She was a fighter! However, the CPO was granted by the uncaring authorities. I stood by them despite the future for their homes not looking good.

It was in 2005 that I joined the local Army Reserves Force (formally the Territorial Army). I really wanted a challenge and to learn new things. I was accepted by the TA (as it was known then) and I became Private Walker. I really enjoyed the weekends away, the training, and pushing myself to the limit (and being pushed sometimes literally to the limit). Going on adventures was fun too. My Section Commanders had dirty mouths, but were not bad people. I never heard our Lord's name taken in vain. I remember one occasion whilst in Lichfield on a training exercise on a class 2 parade early in the morning, I was stood to attention waiting for whoever it was to inspect my uniform. I could not see who it was despite trying to look out of the corner of my eye. When he came to me he said: "Your boots are well polished private." I replied: "Thank you sir." His response was (shouting): "There's no need to call me sir, sergeant will suffice!" On another occasion, I remember being on a PT exercise around 5am, and there was a new leader giving instructions. A fellow reservist stood near me, was told off for something he had or had not done, his reply was "Yes Corporal." There was silence. One of the leaders we did know was a Corporal said: "Corporal? He isn't a Corporal. He is a Senior Military Instructor!" The man addressed as Corporal was in fact an SMI, a warrant officer. It was hard to tell because our leaders were not in uniform, but PT dress, shorts and t-shirts, and when you were standing at attention, you looked straight ahead. I remember on one occasion, one valuable lesson I learned was never feel bad about overstating someone because they can only knock you down to their position, and never understate someone because you are likely to get a telling off! It is like when the Lord Jesus instructed people never to take the high place (Luke 14:10), but be humble. After a few years in the Army Reserves, I was asked on one occasion quite informally by my superior, the officer in charge, if I would I be up for going on a tour of the Middle East for a while and this would be cleared with the police. At first it sounded interesting. He really tried to sell it to me, but there was a catch. The tour would most likely involve very possible conflict if I was to be drafted in, with the very possibility of me losing a limb, limbs or even my life was not out of the question. The limbs, my limbs that were at risk were worth only a few thousand each to the Government so I was informed. My superior in the TA put it very plainly to me like this: "You might need to kill or be killed Walker if you go!" I prayed about this, and realised in my heart that I did not join to go out and kill people or risk losing my life. I was part time, and nothing would be achieved from me killing someone on tour. The conclusion I had made very quickly was I could not have that on my conscience, even live with myself if I ever needed to shoot someone that was intending on killing me or that I could lose a limb without any reassurances of support. This annoyed me in truth so I did the honourable thing and resigned my post with no regrets. My superiors in the TA also understood where I was coming from, and did not blame me. Many others left after me also feeling the armed forces even for part timers were being taken advantage of, and this was the Ministry of Defence doing things on the cheap when willing full time personnel could be used. My dad and my brother Trevor were in the army so it must have been in my blood to give the TA a go.

It was in 2005 that my Aunty Carol (my mam's sister) died. RIP Aunty Carol, I miss you. x. I will always have fond memories of her (especially her homemade chips) and all my family that have passed into the next life all commended to Almighty God through prayer. Life can be unfair, but no one is entitled or guaranteed to great health or a long happy life, but heaven awaits all those that love Almighty God. I know He will not let us down.

Miracles are not just for physical healings

In 2006, Almighty God came to my rescue again. I was in Blackpool on a day out. I had driven there, parked up unknowingly on a private car park that I thought was a free public car park. I enjoyed a lovely day at the seaside, came back to my car to discover I had been clamped. I telephoned the number on the ticket that was placed on my window. Two bulky men turned up and said: "It is going to cost you £95.00 to get released!" I explained that I was sorry, and I did not have £95.00. The men said that if I did not get the money for them in one hour they would tow my car away, and the fine would be much more! I sat down and did not know what to do. I started praying the Divine Mercy prayer that the Lord Jesus Himself promises many unimaginable graces to those who say it:

"Eternal Father, I offer you the body, blood, soul and divinity of your dearly beloved son our Lord Jesus Christ in atonement for our sins, and the sins of the whole world, for the sake of His sorrowful passion have mercy on us and on the whole world." I needed Jesus' help more than ever. I was stranded miles away from Manchester with no money and no access to my own car, and two bulky men were intending to take my car away. In my opinion, what happened next was a complete miracle. The bulky men returned in about half an hour. When I saw them I was thinking what to say because I did not have the money they demanded, but they said "Where do you live?" I said: "Manchester." One man said "We will let you off, but be more careful where you park next time." The bulky men had no idea I had moments earlier asked Jesus for help. Thanks be to Almighty God for His help. What a powerful prayer to God the father, offering His own son back to Him with thanksgiving for all he has done. One of my favourite films would have to be Bruce Almighty. I remember during the film Morgan Freeman who plays God saying: "A miracle is a young person choosing to get an education rather than doing drugs, that's a miracle!" How true that statement is. Miracles of Almighty God are happening all the time, people just do not see them or choose not to see them. It may be the case that you need to be patient. Everything is done in Almighty God's own time. We forget that a thousand years to us could only be a day to Him, so be patient and be persistent in prayer.

In 2008, I took a distance learning course in Life Coaching and obtained a Level 3 Diploma. In 2009, I took a distancing learning course in Private Investing and obtained a Level 4 Diploma, not bad for someone with dyslexia, Almighty God is so gracious! I have included my email address at the end of this book so if I can help or there are any professional opportunities, please do get in touch.

In 2007 that my superiors in the police requested that I moved from Derker to another area that was being targeted by criminals, more than my area was, and therefore more victims. I suppose it is like clergy, there is never any guarantee that one will work in one location forever. There was uproar however from the people of Derker at a public meeting about this when one of my superiors was present representing the force. The local newspaper even wrote about the objections to my transfer. I found this a compliment that the Derker residents would stick up for me like this, but it was out of my hands. To this day, I know the devil himself was behind the move in order to take my regular support for the people of Derker away, especially those who could be made homeless. There was no one official supporting their cause to save their homes only their own little group and me.

I kept in contact with Kath and visited her when I could. I was very saddened to hear that Kath had become unwell and passed away in 2009. I was able to attend her funeral at the Sacred Heart Catholic Church, Derker just a short walk from where she lived. There were no objections from any of my superiors from attending. I knew Almighty God and Kath wanted me there.

The priest said at her funeral: "All Kath wanted to do was leave this earth feeling assured that the authorities did not take her home off her while she was alive - and they didn't!" Kath's family came over from the Netherlands for the funeral, and took ownership of her house that she had left them. It was just the way Kath had wanted before she died. Kath's daughter give me a beautiful wooden cross with Jesus hanging on it. A cross I have on the wall till this day. RIP Kath. I miss you. x

I started work in another part of the Oldham Division, and I enjoyed supporting the residents and monitoring the local criminals there. I was always fair but firm when required. I never had an issue from anyone who regularly broke the law. It was a cat and mouse game to them. They must have enjoyed the thrills at the expense and peace of law abiding residents. Our justice system is not the harshest, in fact it is too soft.

After some years working in GMP, I noticed there was a lot of atheists. The devil was very active working in others that would blaspheme our Lord's name in front of me, no doubt to upset my spirit. This caused my spirit to be very perturbed and this occurred mostly every day. At meal times in the station canteen when we were in there having a break, one colleague would say in mockery, "Are we going to say grace before we eat? Then one would say, "Grace, ha." I think that was said for my benefit. It was no secret that I am a Christian. I was fortunate enough to be offered a key and the use of a room in the community centre on my beat to have my meals and use the facilities there. This was something I prayed for because it was two miles away from my beat to the police station; and I was mostly pounding my area. I thank Almighty God that my prayers were answered. Blasphemy is a big problem today and offends Almighty God immensely. People are loose with what they say, using Almighty God's name as a swear word or disrespectfully. If Almighty God was okay with His creation using His Holy name as they please, He would not have made it one of the "do nots" in the Ten Commandments.

Sadly, my superiors in the police were as equally responsible at times for taking Almighty God's name in vain, this left me feeling often astounded. I raised my concerns, but it fell on deaf ears. What was I to do? I prayed about it. I knew that Almighty

God does not just speak to us in His word and sacrament, but also in our experience. In my heart on one occasion, Almighty God said to my inner most being: **"Simon, make use of available technology, do not be afraid to tell them, what they are saying about me is very wrong, remember I am with you always.** " I recall Deuteronomy 31:6: "Be strong and courageous. Do not be afraid or terrified, for the Lord your God goes with you; He will never leave or forsake you." I hoped and prayed that the blasphemy would stop altogether, but it got even worse every time I was in the station. I could not ignore Almighty God any more, and although out of my comfort zone, I got the message to all to stop blaspheming. This was done via e-mail as I felt Almighty God had told me in my heart. I sent a polite email, but yet again, the devil through my superiors, tried to cause me distress. I was called to the boss's office and with Almighty God's help, I explained my reasons when put under pressure, and soon after it was discovered that it was actually force policy not to take the name of the Lord Jesus Christ in vain. Praise Almighty God I thought, with no surprise, the blasphemy soon stopped. St. Paul reminded me:

"For our struggle is not against flesh and blood, but against the rulers, against the authorities, against the powers of this dark world, and against the spiritual forces in the heavenly places." (Ephesians 6:12).

There was an occasion when I was recruiting for Home Watch members that a resident tried to persuade me to become a free mason. He said if I joined I would never need to worry about my job in the police again, and that I would be rubbing shoulders with all the top brass of the police. I was informed it was a secret organisation that does loads of good work. There is nothing good about doing things in secret. The Lord Jesus did no good work in secret so this is where it falls down. I declined their offer of membership. I worked with some good people in the police who were very passionate about policing and keeping people safe. Sadly, there were a lot of officers that were immature, bragged about extra martial affairs and were governed by pride.

The local Catholic Church on my beat was St. Joseph's. But again, it became difficult for me to attend holy mass because the police briefings would go on sometimes beyond 9am, and mass would have already started. If I was lucky enough, I would get there to receive our Lord Jesus' precious body and blood. The Rev Fr John was very understanding, and knew the predicament I was in. He said: "If you get here on time, great, if not, do not worry, I will always give you our Lord."

In May 2007, after living on my own for nearly 3 years, I started praying to Almighty God about my marital status. If it was His will, I wanted to share

my life and faith with a Catholic lady. I started
corresponding via social media with a lady from the
Philippines named Florgeolette. I had the internet
by then. Florge and I had a lot in common. The
people from Philippines are mostly very devout
Catholics. Florge invited me to visit her and her
family in the Philippines. I had arranged to visit her
in January 2008. We felt we had corresponded for
long enough. It was less than two weeks before I
was to travel to the Philippines that I received a
telephone call from Florge, crying over the phone,
that her youngest sister Ivy had died suddenly from
an asthma attack. What do you say to someone
over the phone on the other side of the world? I
could only say: "I was very sorry." I asked Florge if
she still wanted me to visit and she did. I was happy
just to be with the family, and all the activities she
had previously told me about could be cancelled,
but Florge said that Ivy would want us to carry on
as normal. How could we, I thought, a family in
grief. I visited the Philippines as planned. What
amazed me was the customer service I received
and the great faith in Almighty God people in the
Philippines had, especially Florge and her family. I
could see that although in grief, they trusted that
Ivy, just aged 24 was with her Lord that she was
devoted to and loved. Florge and her family showed
me around Manila and Davao and despite the grief,
we did manage a few laughs. I visited Ivy's resting
place to pay my respects. I was pleased she was

with Our Lord, but I wished I would have met her in person before she went to heaven. I only saw her on the webcam whilst communicating with Florge. I left the Philippines after a couple of weeks, and I kept in touch with Florge online. I visited her again in September 2008, then corresponded with her via email, and visited again in June 2009. Again, some fellow officers in the police office would try and cast doubt on my discernment. One officer said, "Be careful, she is just after a British passport and a better life here." This hurt me, and I knew this was from the devil, so I took no notice. I did not believe the devil's lies. He is the father of lies: (John 8:44). I wondered whether some people were jealous because I was happy. My heart told me that Florge was the one Almighty God had chosen for me, and Almighty God had never let me down previously so why would He now?! If Almighty God can part the Red Sea for His people, He could bless and guide us, I thought. Florge moved to England in October 2009 after giving up everything for me. This is an outward and inward display of love if ever there was one. To this day, this is very difficult for me to take in - that someone could give up everything for me, and not that she would be any better off with me. She had everything she needed and could ever have wanted in the Philippines. Florge is the full package for me. Not only is she internally and externally a beautiful person, but she is also extremely holy and well educated. She comes from a family of judges and barristers. One thing I learned from my first visit was that Florge's family love a good debate. I thought they were always arguing at first in a language alien to me! Florge possesses a wonderful gentle spirituality, but she is not to be messed with. She has such a strong character, as do I. I think we complement each other to be honest. Florge has been my gift from Almighty God, and I pray that Almighty God will help me be a better husband each day. Florge has many talents. One of them is cooking, in particular Filipino dishes.

My favourite dishes would have to be Nilaga and Adobo, pork or chicken, for any Filipinos reading this, will be familiar with these dishes.

I have never been too concerned of the kind of food I eat because the Lord Jesus makes it quite clear in His word that it is what comes out of a person that makes him/her unclean; not what goes into a person (Mark 7:15). A balanced diet is important however.

The planning of our wedding was not too difficult. We were not out to impress anyone, although Florge was very fortunate to have her flowers on the day. We had ordered them personally at the florist two weeks before, however, the day before our wedding, we went to collect them. They were not even ordered. The lady had put our order behind others' papers on the notice board and it was forgotten about. The lady could not apologise enough and said, "You are very calm about this?" I said, "What good would it do shouting and arguing with you?" The lady gave Florge some different flowers, but Florge was not too fussy.

Sadly, this has been my general experience with the customer service in England in recent years, but Almighty God has helped me not to expect too much and to realise I will end up very disappointed if I do expect too much.

Florge and I were married at 1pm on the 23rd January 2010 at Christ the King Catholic Church, Newton Heath, Manchester. We were blessed with a bright and dry day.

There were 50 guests that attended our wedding including, family, relatives, relations, and a few friends. We had a solemn marriage ceremony, and a holy mass offered for us both. Afterwards we had a lovely buffet in the Dean Brook pub just a short distance away from the church. At the reception we played some games, and had some karaoke. Paul and Trevor were too shy to speak for me but everyone seemed to have a great time.

We remembered what Almighty God said in His word about being inclusive when you host a party (Luke14:12) all walks of life were at our wedding. Some were fighting life's struggles of their own, but there was a great sense of tangible joy and happiness from everyone. Florge and I enjoyed a short break in London for our honeymoon. My sister-in-law, Hayley who works in the industry was able to get us a good deal in a hotel. I was back in work after a couple of weeks.

We had arranged to renew our wedding vows in the Philippines in December 2010 for Florge's family because they were unable to attend our wedding in England. I believe the devil tried to stop us doing this. Firstly our flight was delayed for two days, and our luggage had got lost that we were without for eight days. At the time, it was frustrating to arrive so far away from home with only the things we were stood up in, no towel, nothing. After reflecting and we knew that Almighty God had taught us a valuable lesson through the devil's attack, causing staff to be incompetent. What must it be like for those enduring without the basic needs every day? The inconvenience became a blessing to us. There are people in the Philippines who are poor. We counted our blessings. We had a lovely time in the Philippines. The people there are so caring and friendly. Nothing is too much trouble for them, from the airport staff, taxi drivers, shop workers etc. I was very impressed that so many Filipinos have such strong faith in the Lord Jesus. The Philippines is a nation that suffers greatly from all kinds of problems, yet despite this, the people never give up or lose faith in Almighty God. They are so resilient, always having their heads held high.

I remember visiting some of Florge's relatives one year that were victims of a natural disaster. I have never seen anything quite like it. Massive trees in half on the ground. Almighty God does not promise us an easy life but we need not worry. He will never leave us and all this is temporary. We have no claim on Almighty God. The Filipino people have such amazing endurance and resilience. I would say their motto for life is this:

Anxious In Nothing

Prayerful In Everything

Thankful For Anything

Florge and I after the renewal of our vows in Davao, Philippines

Blessing Florge's mam, a tradition and mark of respect in the Philippines

RIP Mrs Omelio (2012) Rise in Glory!

Florge and I with Mr & Mrs Omelio

Renewing of our wedding vows overlooking the sea

We arrived at the airport ready for our long flight home, and were informed we were not even on the flight! To our knowledge, we were scheduled to fly from Manila, China, Paris then Manchester. The man at the airport very dismissively said, "You are not on this flight, sorry." I thought it was a joke or a dream. To make matters worse we were informed that we would need to pay again, and we were out of funds. The flight that we should have been on was closing its gate, and we felt totally abandoned. This was a horrible feeling. The reality we were in was very stressful. We discovered that when the lady at Manchester was rebooking us on this flight, due to the adverse weather, she had omitted to register us on our return flight from Manila. Florge and I looked at each other trying to take in what was going on. I called in the flight office with very little hope. It was a stressful time. Then out of nowhere the lady in the airport office came out and gently said: "Hello Mr Walker, I have put you both on a flight to Amsterdam, is that okay?" Florge and I made a big sigh of relief. We had worried for nothing. Our Lord had it all planned. The airport in Manila has its own Catholic chapel with Our Lord present in the tabernacle. I went in and cried, not just because I was relieved, but because I was sorry and doubted Him. As I prayed, the words to the song 'He's got the whole world in His hands' came to my mind. Almighty God showed me that He does have everything under His control. I apologised to Almighty God for doubting Him, and felt His wonderful peace cover me.

I would describe Florge's and my life as quite ordinary, and we supported each other well in the faith serving the Lord. In February 2011, we both decided to increase our number, and we would try for a family. Florge quickly conceived, and thanks to Almighty God she did not have any morning sickness. Florge was given her due date for early November 2011. We were to keep the gender a secret from ourselves, and decided that if we were having a boy, he would be called Campion after St. Campion or Trezelle Ivy after St. Trezelle of France if we were having a girl.

It was in March 2011 that Florge's life and my life could have changed for the worse. I was invited to a birthday party in Manchester by my friend, Mark. I discussed it with Florge who encouraged me to attend, so I did. Going to night clubs and pubs was a thing of the past for me, and I had experienced regrettably my share of pointless hangovers having drank too much. Anyway, that night, I attended. I had only consumed a couple of beers when my mobile phone rang. It was Florge telephoning me. She sounded very concern and distressed as she informed me when she visited the toilet she was bleeding, and thought she was having a miscarriage. I quickly informed my friend Mark about this, and told him I would be leaving. I left the pub, phoned my parents, and arranged to be collected. My mam also kindly drove us to the North Manchester General Hospital. Florge was to undergo blood tests etc. and we were being prepared for the worse possible news by the specialists that our baby might be gone. We just sat there for around 4 hours. We were all praying and tearful. We hoped and prayed that Almighty God in His goodness would not take our baby to Himself, and that all would be well. After several hours in the hospital we were given the news we wanted to hear. Florge and our baby were going to be fine, and there was nothing to worry about – Thanks to Almighty God! The specialist said bleeding is not a common thing with early pregnancies, but it happens. That child of ours was here to stay and thanks be Almighty God for this.

The busiest shift when I was working for the police would be in the evenings as there would be an increase in anti-social behaviour, as the children would have finished school. The residents on my beat would phone up complaining about groups of young people hanging about etc. When I was on an early shift, I could make arrangements to swap my shift in order to accompany Florge to the antenatal clinic at the North Manchester General Hospital. It was in my superior's interest to allow me to do this as in the evenings the numbers were needed to deal with the calls that came in, anti-social behaviour etc.

It was a lovely feeling being at the antenatal ward. Florge was being closely monitored, not only because of the previous scare, but also because she has type 2 diabetes. We were appointed a specialist diabetic midwife called Helena. Helena could not do enough for us. Florge had a scan at 5 weeks. The medical technology was amazing I thought. At Florge's 5 weeks scan, we could see the tiny heartbeat of our baby. The gender was to be a surprise.

We thought about how many innocent lives are deliberately and directly killed in the womb all over the world. In England alone there are over 203,000 killed per year and that figure is rising. Many babies at that time of their death no older than 5 weeks (as ours was) in their mother's womb, innocent yet rejected just for existing, some wombs are no longer the safest place for the unborn as they should be. "Everyone who is for abortion is already born," wise words from the late U.S President Ronald Regan. His statement is so very true, yet many ignore this. Why does any baby deserve their life taking from them and to be put to death? Where are the rights for the unborn?

There was a news report on 24th March 2014 that stated that the medical director in the NHS was writing to all hospitals reminding them that it is illegal to burn aborted babies as clinical waste. How sad it is not illegal to kill unborn babies! It is perfectly legal to take the life of an unborn baby, but the way a dead unborn baby is disposed of is illegal. The health authorities prefer to use the word "foetus," That word is probably easier on their consciences.

In fact, the Holy Spirit has informed me that abortion is one, if not the greatest evils in the world today so do not let anyone bluff you about it. The devil is behind it all, from teaching doctors to perform them to blinding politicians to pass and approve abortion as legal and acceptable, and it is such a massive profitable business. Even the terminology used by the abortionists about abortion comes across like it is no big deal: "….. It is the ending of a pregnancy so that there will not be any baby." Nothing said about the taking of innocent lives. There is no going back once a baby is killed, he/she is irreplaceable. The devil has and is fooling all here if you believe his lies that abortion is not murder – the devil is the father of lies the Lord Jesus tells us: (John 8:44). The Lord Jesus saw the devil fall like lightening from heaven because he is a murderer and a liar (Luke 10:18). I wholeheartedly support the work of the pro-life movements, and pray that those entrusted with safeguarding the unborn will do so instead of turning against them. The Lord Jesus makes it very clear that "If anyone sins against a little one, it would be better for him/her to wrap a millstone around their neck, and be thrown into the deep sea!" (Matthew 18:6). Anyway, Florge would have further scans at 12 weeks, 20 weeks and 28 weeks and thank God for an overall stress free pregnancy. I would look forward to Florge's monthly update each month of her pregnancy and what was new with our baby's development. The 4D scan was the last of the scans.

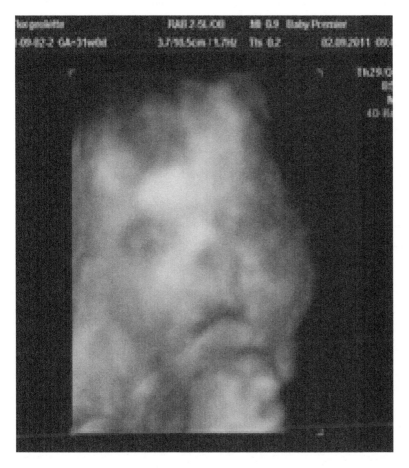

The 31 weeks 4D scan of a baby (not a foetus) boy or a girl?

Since I moved into our home in 2004, I had not made many alternations or modifications, and our home could have done with it by 2011. For me, home was a place to keep dry, shower and sleep. The carpets were clean but had been down for years. Florge rightly so said we needed changes for our new family member. Having never really been materialistic regards goods, I was able to save the money I earned reasonably well. I used the money I had saved, and over a short time our home had a new look and I have to say became a nicer place and cosy. My mam had also told me that every home needed a "woman's touch." Thanks to Florge our home has this now.

My journey following the Lord Jesus has been no walk in the park. I do not know a Christian that has had it plain sailing. I struggled with the devil who would continue to cause me trouble in any way he could. The devil knows our individual weaknesses and will try and lead us to sin with the help of the other fallen angels and go against Almighty God. The devil's job is to make us feel bad and give up. No doubt all Christians face this daily. Our commitment to the Lord Jesus is on a daily basis. Every day is a bonus an old priest once told me, Fr Timothy it was (RIP). A day to be better than the previous day. In football, if you listen you can often on the pitch hear the words "Start again." The players mean they will begin a new attack to try and score from the defence and work their way up the field. This is the case with faith and our relationship with Almighty God. We will not always get things right and slip up occasionally by saying or doing something we later regret, but we must start again, and not beat ourselves up spiritually. Almighty God's enemy, the devil, tried this on me on many occasions and to cause me upset. One way the devil did this was through my superiors in the police. There were some police employees I believe, and through pride that were still vexed by my email when I called for the blasphemy to stop. On one occasion, one superior accused me of not attending two appointments that had been arranged for me, at a school and with a resident. He said that I was letting the police down. Thanks be to Almighty God I could prove I had attended, but there was never an apology from my superiors. Pride gets in the way a lot, I thought. On another occasion, I was reported for carrying carrier bags of shopping on duty, little did anyone know, I was bringing in provisions for my friend Kath who was elderly and had poor mobility.

From my early days as a Christian, I recalled what Our Lord said to His followers: **"I am sending you out like sheep among wolves. Therefore be as wise as serpents and as gentle as doves."** (Matthew 10:16). I would always ask God to cover my back, walk in front and at the side of me. My police pocket notebook was always signed by the victim whenever I visited them as proof I had personally attended to provide reassurance and crime prevention advice. The Holy Bible warned me often: **"Be alert and sober, your enemy the devil roars around like a lion, looking for someone to devour"** (1Peter 5:8). I needed to be alert on every shift in the police. I have written enough already about my experiences in the police, but there is just a little more to tell you. I did mix and engage with police colleagues, but it was very difficult as only a handful had good spirits in them. I want to stay on track giving thanks to Almighty God. It is important however for you, the reader, to know my experiences, and what Almighty God in His goodness has done to guard and guide my life. The life of me, a poor sinner that deserves nothing from Almighty God.

When I was not in the police office, I found myself a free spirit and helping the residents on my beat. You should know that one superior named me in front of others: "The man of mystery." This was because I would be out of the office for long periods, working hard, often in the faces of the local criminals, simply doing the job I was paid to do. I was not waiting to be asked to do the work by superiors as some would. The Holy Spirit put in my heart that it was the devil that would always put suspicion in the minds of my superiors. There were some colleagues that would happily sit back and let me take the jobs on when they came in; and if they were friendly with the supervisors, revel in doing much less than me. What they did not know is that it was with Almighty God's help and for Almighty God's service that I worked hard. At times I was not such a free spirit when I needed to be in the office. Even for only a short time, it was awful, even though I was polite and civil with everyone. I was faced with and in the presence of so much arrogance, insensitivity and immaturity. It is amazing how people behave when given a bit of authority. My spirit of peace was under attack. I would need to get my work done in the office as I would be required to put data on the police system. There were many colleagues that although did not take the Lord God's name in vain would speak with bad taste, use filthy language, and talk about intimate things and brag about their actions even those that were married. I regret not being bolder speaking out against the immaturity and the evil, but I suppose I did not want the environment becoming more difficult to work in. There were some officers that would try and bring me into their unsavoury conversations knowing full well the topics were against my spirit. Our Lord warns us in His holy word about gossiping. This was another battle I faced in employment including in the police - the gossip! My brother worked with the husband of an officer I worked with, and he would tell my brother things that were said about me and work that could have only come from his wife, dear reader, you get the picture.

The police office was not the environment I enjoyed working in, but with Almighty God's help I carried on. I was given the strength to get on with it and focus on supporting those that needed me in the community. I spent long hours on foot in the police, and subsequently I became a sufferer of "policeman's heel." The medical term is Plantar Fasciitis. Anyone that has had it will know it is a very painful foot condition. I was under the Podiatrist receiving regular treatment. I would often use the bike at work and cycle around my beat to take the pressure off foot patrolling. I would often walk several miles each duty that was between 8-10 hours long. When my condition became common knowledge in the police office, suddenly the bike that I had no problem using many times previously became difficult to use as officers would take it out of the bike shed and use it themselves. I would be left with the bike that was too small for me or the one in the shed waiting to be collected because it was unsafe and needed fixing or had a flat tyre.

One of my superiors sent an email out to everyone stating "..... Revert to walking if your bike is not there in the bike shed!!" The Holy Spirit informed me that although this message was sent to everyone, this was directed at me. The devil had used him. I did not need an email like that. It certainly did not improve my condition. I became very annoyed with the superiors' complete lack of sensitivity and it started to get to me. I knew the devil himself was behind it. I was not the type of person to go off sick, but I was in pain. I prayed hard to God to help me, and I always remembered His promise to me from a young age that **He will never abandon me**. (Hebrews 13:5). With Almighty God's help, I carried on, and cycled when I could. I prayed that if it be Almighty God's will He would help me find another job. By now I was at my wits end! I was to endure several more months that I detested it, to be honest. Of course there were some good officers, but many where not nice and arrogant. I informed Almighty God about all this, and He acted and answered a poor sinner like me. How great Almighty God is.

One Thursday in July 2011, I was on my day off. Florge was getting bigger now in her pregnancy, our baby was growing fast. Florge was still at work but was on lighter duties by now. This particular day, I dropped her off and picked her up from work. Florge would always pick up the Manchester Evening News paper for me.

That evening as I was reading the job section, I noticed a job in there that caught my eye. Xaverian College in Manchester were advertising for a College Community Support Coordinator, like the

Head of Security. The job would entail me to promote a harmonious community, promote high standards of conduct, and address any forms of anti- social behaviour, dealing with official visitors, non-official visitors as well as other duties, including liaising with local police etc. I thought this would be right down my street, no day would be the same, such variety. It could be my lease of life from Almighty God, like I had been asking for. I did some research about Xaverian College in Manchester.

I discovered its origins were from the Xaverian Brothers - a religious order founded in honour and memory of St. Francis Xavier who was the first Jesuit missionary. The Xaverian Brothers, in various locations came to Bury, Greater Manchester in the 1800's to offer education to the poor that would otherwise have struggled to be educated without privilege. The Xaverian Brothers came to Victoria Park in Manchester in 1907, its current location.

I thought and prayed about this opportunity. Could I continue with the misery I was experiencing in the police force? And as a future dad, I knew the hours in the police force would not be ideal as I would be working shifts I would only end up seeing my child at varied times, when he/she was sleeping? I had nothing to lose I thought, so I asked for an application form. I remember saying, "Lord, this would be perfect for me. I will be helping people in need, and I would be able to worship you and receive you at mass every day during my break. Please, if it is your holy will let me work there." I received my application form, and carefully filled it in. I said to my wife that. "I am really going to sell myself here." I included a personal statement to support my application. I was so desperate at this stage to leave GMP, and felt I had put up with enough. Anyway, soon after applying, I received a reply from Xaverian College inviting me to attend an interview. My interview was at 12.15pm. I checked my diary, and the rota I was working was 4pm-12am. Praise God I said. I do not even need to inform anyone in the police. If they knew I had an interview and I was unsuccessful, I would be the centre of the regular small talk for a while, and I just did not need it. The day of the interview came and I was really nervous. I dressed in a suit with shirt and tie, and brought my police uniform and boots with me. I could get changed in the car after my interview ready for my 4pm start. I was early. I signed in at reception and was given a visitors badge. I was first met by the Vice Principal Mr Knowles. He informed me that I was to be shown around the college first by him, then given a task, and then interviewed by three members of the senior management team. I listened intently as Mr Knowles explained the history of Xaverian and the different buildings within the campus. I was quiet throughout the tour trying to take in what I was being told. I thought I was going to be quizzed about it, like what would be the quickest way from one building to another?! The tour from Mr Knowles was very interesting and informative. Mr Knowles informed me he had been at Xaverian for many years. I thought about the great work the brothers and staff had done all those years educating and ministering to the people of Manchester. I did my task answering different scenarios on a question paper, and then finally was interviewed by the college Principal Mrs Hunter, and two Assistant Principals. I was very nervous as this interview had been my first interview in years. The interview was in the Principal's office. To this day, I have always felt uneasy in places of authority, but although there was a big table for meetings etc., I saw a crucifix on the wall that I kept glancing at during the interview asking Almighty God to help me say the right things. This comforted me greatly throughout the interview. I felt a wonderful peace at the interview. I was informed this was a new role within the college. I answered the questions as honestly as I could and we said our farewells. I was informed by the Principal that I would receive a phone call at 4pm that day with the result of my interview – successful or not. I was hoping so much to be successful.

I got in my car and got changed there with a bit of difficulty, and I drove to work for my 4pm start. I put the college's phone number in my phone so I would know who it was when they called. At 4pm in the police office, I started feeling uncomfortable because I knew that once the police briefing had started, no phones were allowed. I prayed and I know it was Almighty God that prevented the police briefing not starting on time. There were officers including superiors messing around. I had already put my phone on silent ready for the police briefing. I felt my phone ring, it was Xaverian College and Mrs Hunter spoke: "Hello Simon, Mrs Hunter here, how do you think it went today?" I said: "I was nervous Mrs Hunter, but I did my best." Mrs Hunter said: "Your best is good enough Simon. We would like to offer you the job." Well, I was filled with so much happiness and joy. Words cannot describe it, and yes dear reader, I accepted right away over the phone. I would need to hand in a months' notice I thought, and take any holidays owed to me. The police briefing was called at 4.10pm (how Almighty God plans these things I thought). It was the best police briefing I have ever been in. I knew it was the work of Almighty God, and all my prayers were answered. My perseverance had paid off. At first, I only shared the news with a couple of colleagues, and then it became police office knowledge. I said my farewells. I had no regrets for joining GMP but my last year was not pleasant so I have no regrets for resigning. I did leave GMP though feeling very confused that the staff would speak ill of Jesus' holy name, yet left every other faith alone. I was given a leaving present and I just said a simple "Thanks."

The leaving present was not much after servicing for 7 and half years, and putting into everyone's collections whatever they were for. Almighty God worked very powerfully in this situation though, I received a lovely character reference from Human Resources. I realised how fortunate and blessed I am to be out of the police office and it was time to move on. The highlight of my career in the police was returning lost children to their families and working on Operation Purple 7. I worked with Princess Anne, the Princess Royal's protection officers. Princess Anne had an engagement in Bury, and would be driven to Clayton Playing fields, near the Oldham Athletic ground. She would get out of a car, walk to the field and board a waiting helicopter. It was a good job Princess Anne had boots on, the field was very muddy. I enjoyed that experience. Overall, staff in the police office were not bad people, but many were atheists and never had any regards for the holy name of Jesus. It serves as a good reminder to me, especially that:

"If one loves Jesus, the people of the world will hate you" (Matthew 10:22).

My experience as a Christian in the work place was a tough one, and what the Lord Jesus tells me was true for me, not because of anything I had done, but because I love the Lord Jesus. I could never compare myself to other Christians that are being tortured and killed because of their love and belief in the Lord Jesus.

And so, a new chapter began in my life. I was and am very grateful to Mrs Hunter (or Mary as she liked to be called) and the Xaverian Community for having faith in me and giving me the job. I started my new job at Xaverian College, based in Student Services on 26th September 2011. My first day, my induction and like with any job was about getting to know people and settling in. I found everyone very friendly, and it had a great sense of family community and faith. I would be dealing with different things just like when I worked in the police, but Jesus and His holy name was held in high regard. I would be everything to everyone, from someone reporting that their phone was lost, to me looking after visitors at reception. I feel very blessed working here, and I have received so much support even from the Learning Support Department that kindly gave me an overlay to assist me in my reading (remember the difficulties I had with looking at the words on the page and it becoming fuzzy writing?) Since having the overlay I have been able to read without any problems. Thank God. It is a condition known as meares irlen syndrome. I only wish this difficulty would have been detected when I was younger, but all in Almighty God's perfect timing.

Anyway I had just started at Xaverian College. I worked Monday, Tuesday, and Wednesday finding my way around, and then Florge and my life were to change forever. I attended Aikido on Wednesday evening as usual, and had just arrived home from the lesson. As I walked through the front door, Florge shouted from the bathroom "I have heard something pop just now." Florge phoned the hospital. It was 11pm and we were advised to go to North Manchester General Hospital (NMGH) for tests. It was only that very day in the morning, Florge had packed her hospital bag ready for in 5 weeks' time when she was due to give birth in November. The window blinds had also been put up, and the house was complete ready for our new baby. We arrived at NMGH and Florge had some tests. I stayed with her throughout and sat in a chair. The specialist informed us that Florge was 6cms towards being fully dilated, in simple terms, she was already in labour. I was informed that I was going to become a dad in the very near future. Florge and I were taken to the labour ward. Florge was given an epidural, and as I helped the specialist support Florge's weight, and she leaned on me, I felt a twinge in my own back! I said: "my back hurts." This gave everyone a smile looking after us. We had prayed previously that Almighty God in His goodness would grant us very caring staff, and we could not have asked for anyone better. There was an Asian specialist wearing glasses examining Florge and he said: "You have a big baby Mr Walker to say she is 5 weeks early." I found his comments reassuring. Things started to happen, and I became more awake. I was sat in a chair throughout. I was groggy and hungry but I did not want to leave in case our baby came and I was not there. There are no rehearsals. At 10.30am, Florge said: "Use my phone, and take some pictures." We had left the camera at home, not thinking Florge was in labour and would give birth within hours! At 11.16am on Thursday 29th September 2011 (Feast of the Archangels).

Our baby was born, 6.2lbs. I was in floods of tears of joy as she was delivered. I tried to take photos, and just about managed it with Florge's phone. We had had a baby girl: Trezelle Ivy. I had never felt the Holy Spirit of God quite like that when my Trezelle was born. Florge and I did a little research on St. Trezelle of France, her full name was Mary (Maria) Gabriel Trezelle.

Gabriel is an Archangel of Almighty God, and our beautiful daughter was born 5 weeks early on the feast of the Archangels, that was just wonderful! For us – God instance not coincidence.

A tired me, holding my Trezelle minutes after she was born on 29th Sept 2011, 11.16am

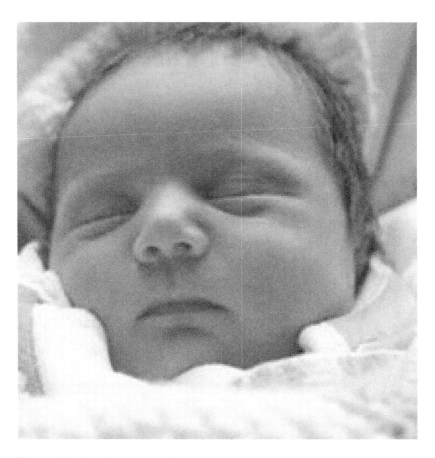

Trezelle having a well needed sleep just hours after being born

I was informed by the specialists that Florge and Trezelle needed to stay in hospital for a few days and be monitored for Florge's sugar levels and Trezelle because she was premature and she had quite a lot of jaundice. Florge was transferred to the post-natal ward and Trezelle to the neo-natal ward.

I went home on that Thursday, showered and had the best sleep ever. I was refreshed and returned back to the hospital later that afternoon. I was the most excited man in the world. Every couple of hours Florge needed to visit Trezelle for breastfeeding and bonding. I went back to work at Xaverian College on that Monday. Florge and Trezelle had been in hospital for a few nights now. I was shopping in Asda and was planning to visit them and bring in some provisions that evening. Anyway, I was near the dairy aisle in Asda when I saw an Asian man wearing glasses with a tall teenage lad (I assumed he was his son). I recognised his face (I had never been bad with recognising faces) and I said: "Excuse me, but are you a doctor on the NICU at North Manchester?" He smiled and said: "Yes, I am. How do you know me?" I said: "You looked after my Trezelle." He replied: "Oh yes, how could I forget Trezelle, such a big baby!" The doctor had commented that for a baby at 34 weeks plus 6 days she was bigger than most, who are mostly under 4 pounds. The Asda I was in was massive. I believe it was not by coincidence that our paths crossed again in such a big place, but Almighty God's will, and it gave me another opportunity to say thanks to the doctor again. How Almighty God in His goodness gives different people all these gifts and talents, I thought.

The doctor, whose name I did not get must have cared for some really tiny babies. On Trezelle's ward, there were some really tiny babies, so cute and yet full of confidence. They were so helpless yet knew actually what they wanted - feeding, changing, and no one was going to keep them quiet until their needs were met! I wonder how those other babies are doing today. After 6 days, I could finally bring Florge and Trezelle home.

There was not just a card and chocolates to buy for the labour ward, but also the Antenatal and Neonatal wards. Everyone was marvellous with us, and our prayers were answered, we had professional and caring staff. Everything was in place for our new arrival –Trezelle Ivy.

How wonderful God is. Trezelle soon settled in her new home and was in a routine. Almighty God brought me to Xaverian College, but I could not wait to finish my shift, and get home to be with the family.

The first few weeks with Trezelle

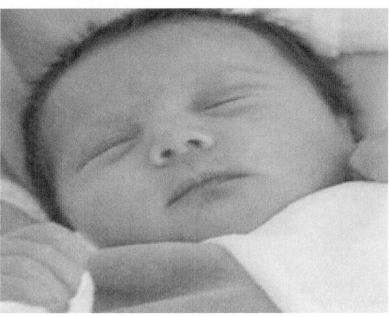

Trezelle's 1st Christmas with Nana & Grandad Walker in 2011. Trezelle adores her Nana & Grandad.

Trezelle's first Christmas in 2011

As devote Catholic parents, it was very important to us that our daughter Trezelle became a child of Almighty God and for the stain of original sin to be washed away from her soul. To have Trezelle baptised was a priority, but I should point out for the right reasons, not simply for a place in a catholic school as sadly is often the case today.

A lukewarm commitment to the Lord Jesus is just not good enough. Jesus is never lukewarm with us even though we are all sinners! A weekly visit on His day (Sunday) to Jesus' house should be the absolute minimum He receives from people.

At Trezelle's Baptism on 22ⁿᵈ January 2012

Christ the King Church where we were married 1 day short of 2 years before.

Trezelle with mummy

Florge is a great role model for Trezelle. If Trezelle becomes even half of the person my wife is, she would have done well.

One of my many interests is gardening so why not introduce this hobby of mine to Trezelle. "As long as it is not too cold or wet!" Florge would say! Thank be to Almighty God for giving us a garden. We have a duty to care for it.

Over the years, I have seen so many not give their garden the respect it deserves, simply by neglecting it and there are many people living in high storey flats that would only love a garden to enjoy – crazy it is!

The Lord Jesus is His goodness has help me understand that not everyone has the same mentality. We are to pray that we will be given the strength to persevere and be patient with others just like He and they are with us. We are no just commanded to love God with all our minds, hearts and souls, but our neighbours as well.

"A new command I give you: Love one another. As I have loved you, so you must love one another. By this everyone will know that you are my disciples, if you love one another."   (John 13:34-35).

Trezelle has always accompanied her mum and me to mass every Sunday .Trezelle often says: "Hi Jesus, Jesus is alive! And "Hi Mummy Mary." On 29th September 2020, Trezelle was 9 years old. She is very bright and we are very proud of her. May God continue to bless her and may Our Blessed Lady wrap her immaculate mantle around her. Amen. Almighty God is so wonderful.

In June 2012, attending a friend's wedding

You have read about the good news in our lives. Now I must turn your attention to things that are not so good, not in our lives, but in the world.

I do not need to inform you the reader that the world is in a terrible state, but for the record - I will do! This is mainly because human beings on the whole have no regard for Almighty God and very little regard for His laws. Generally people prefer to live their own way and not Almighty God's way. The world is very secular, hostile, ruthless, and arrogant as well as other things. There are nations that disobey Almighty God, groups disobey Almighty God, families disobey Almighty God, and individuals disobey Almighty God without any fear that He is watching them or that they will be held to account. I have given too much attention to the devil already than I wanted to, but it is important that you the reader is made aware of his existence and his ways. The devil is very committed to pulling the wool over people's eyes. He does not want people to believe in Almighty God and he tries very hard to convince them Almighty God is just made up fiction. And the devil does not want anyone to know he exists and is working against God and for evil in the world. The devil hates Almighty God's mercy that is freely offered to those that accept it. Sadly, there are so many that refuse Almighty God's invitation. Let us look at what is wrong with the world. The world is beautiful, it is what human beings are doing in it that is the problem!

The greatest gift Almighty God gives His creation is life. The devil's work includes promoting death by killings whether it is in war, when humans have failed to talk and negotiate, and will kill each other at any cost, and the ending of lives with abortions. It saddened me to hear evil declared against the innocent unborn. The unborn are human with potential. We also have the promoting of euthanasia and assisted suicide and even promoting this for children to have their lives taken by adults that should be safeguarding them. This is the terrible situation with laws passed in Belgium and others. No doubt more countries will follow suit with this evil from the devil despite the protests against it.

The Government in this country, as well as in other countries, focuses too much on what is illegal and not what is against Almighty God, immoral and wrong.

I feel inspired to write about the following that is close to my heart.

The Environment and Littering

We do not own this planet, we are stewards and stewardesses. Almighty God owns this planet. We have a duty to look after His world and this includes putting rubbish and waste in the bin and recycling properly.

Food

Did you know that the food and slimming industry is worth millions each year and yet so many people struggle to get enough nourishment? I am sure you do. There are 7 million tonnes of food and drink (nearly 50%) thrown away each year in the UK whilst more than ever, hard pressed families rely on hand-outs from food banks to fill their stomachs. Often on the news we are constantly reminded that England is becoming more and more obese, and yet hundreds of take away menus are put through our letterboxes every year. What madness goes on in our world.

Dear reader, please always give thanks to Almighty God before and after meal times for what has been provided for you.

Divorce and family break-ups

The devil also works tirelessly breaking families up. Satan loves chaos in family life. According to the Office for National Statistics in England and Wales for 2012, there were 118,140 divorces in England and Wales or 13 divorces an hour. It is furthermore expected that 42% of marriages will end in divorce in the future. I have driven passed solicitors with a big sign in their window offering a divorce package for a one off fee! Just how easy human beings easily undo what God has put together (Matthew 19:6). Divorce is reserved for the worst-case scenarios – adultery, abuse in many forms: physical, verbal maltreatment, injury assault, violation, rape, unjust practices, crimes or other aggression. When we lived in a world that is ruthless and unforgiving and people use their freewill in this way, it is not surprising that there is very little reconciliation or none at all. A priest friend of mine once said in his weekly newsletter for the 4th Sunday of Lent in 2015 regards to marriage: "The attempt to make Marriage something it is not and can never be, will become another hammer to hit the Church with. We will be accused of all kinds of discriminations and phobias, but it is the enemy the devil who has distorted reality. These powerful and influential forces released in the Western World are deeply disordered and evil and will not result in people's happiness. A society which rejects the Divine Plan for Marriage will find itself with no unit of formation for the children. Lack of marriage has created mayhem for the young who are abandoned by the adults as they walk off into yet another relationship." Fr continues – "How our generation mocks and laughs at Almighty God's law and his Messengers. We will win my dear people as long as we do not sign up to the modern agenda and become like the non-believers. We belong to the Catholic and Apostolic and Roman Church and our head is a fearless and wonderful Shepherd and his name is Francis and he is Christ's Vicar on earth and he speaks Christ's truth to the nations. We must take heed and be counted among those who belong to Christ's flock." Very strong and direct words from the priest that will not sit comfortably with some readers.

Our bodies are temples

Our bodies are the temple for the Holy Spirit who dwells within us.

Therefore we have a duty to look after our bodies. We should not abuse our bodies with cigarettes and too much alcohol and eat healthy fresh foods when possible. We have freewill to make healthy or unhealthy choices. We have a duty to look after our health and the health of others.

"Or do you not know that your body is a temple of the Holy Spirit within you, whom you have from God? You are not your own, for you were bought with a price. So glorify God in your body." 1 Corinthians 6:19-20

Gambling to excess and money

Many people enjoy a harmless flutter, but there are many that gamble to excess having no control over what they are doing until all their money is gone. Some people will even take out loans to gamble to try and win their money back, and risk losing everything even their homes. The lives of gamblers are not just affected, but their families and friends as well. Like most, I enjoy a little flutter on the football coupon or the horses, but when I say a little flutter, I mean pennies. I remember being in a betting shop on one occasion watching the dog racing when a very strange thing happened. There was 6 dogs set to run. I decided to have a few pennies on Trap 1 at a price of 12/1. Anyway, the race started and Trap 1 was leading by some distance, I thought it was a winner. I said to my friend Bert: "The Lord is on that, I am winning!" Suddenly, the dog stopped still, turned around looking back, and others overtook it, and mine ended up finishing last!

Although having a flutter can be fun, Almighty God plays no part in it, and as Almighty God said to my

Godfather Albert, when for him gambling and wasting money was becoming a problem: "**It is a fool's game**."

There are other problems with money as well. We are a nation where people as a whole owe millions of pounds of debt yet people are in the business of loaning money expecting repayments with massive interest rates added, have never had it so good. People often find themselves financially ruined with no means to pay. Members of Parliament in the UK and further afield also have a lot to answer for when claiming and receiving vast amounts of taxpayers money they should not have claimed for, yet received and spent. The scandal with the banks, the list of issues goes on. I need not add anything more to the public knowledge of corruption involved in finance, but Almighty God sees it all and misses nothing, even though the accused believe there is no accountability. No wonder our Lord said you cannot serve both God and money (Luke 16:13) and that it would not be easy for someone who was rich and only centred on money to enter the kingdom of heaven. (Matthew 19:23).

Forgiveness

In 2014 marked the 30th anniversary of the U.K miner's strike. I was not even a teenager then, but I know that it was a massive walk out involving thousands of miners, and the police were drafted in from all over because of the protests and unrest. Those that are old enough to remember will know that not everyone went on strike, but worked in the mines for their own reasons. They were escorted by the police for their own safety. They went against the National Union of Mine workers, and were loathed by those on strike. What is very sad, is that today, over 30 years on, there are still fathers and sons, extended families, friends etc. that hold grudges, do not speak, or offer no forgiveness to each other because of their differences whether they worked or went on strike. This is not pleasing to Almighty God. This is an example with a big problem in our world today, ruthlessness and a lack of forgiveness. It has made our world a worse place. The Lord Jesus makes it very clear about forgiveness. When Peter asked the Lord Jesus: "How many times must I forgive 7 times?" The Lord Jesus replied: "I tell you 77 times." Forgiveness needs to be a continuation and indefinitely. This is what The Lord Jesus is commanding not simply advising each of us to do, but commanding. He commands we forgive because if we do not forgive, we are the first victim. Almighty God will not forgive us. How can any of us expect Him to forgive us our wrongdoings if we do not forgive? In life we all go through difficulties with each other, and not everyone is our cup of tea, some people push our patience to the limit, annoy us, devalue us, and do evil against us, just look at my life as an example of receiving my fair share of poor treatment. There are some very big things that people would say should never be forgiven. I think it is only with Almighty God's help we can truly forgive others especially our enemies. It is Almighty God that gives each of us the ability to forgive the hurts that are caused, and make the way clear for His healing in our hearts. If we do not forgive and deal with the resentment, in short do our bit, we are responsible for blocking the process of Almighty God's wonderful mercy working in our lives. Forgiveness does not happen overnight, and some things are harder to forgive than others, but we are called to work at it and be free. The Lord's Prayer includes: "Forgive us our sins as we forgive those who have sinned against us….." When we say this prayer, we are supposed to mean it, and Almighty God takes us at our word. We are pleading for forgiveness by Him, and we are saying we have forgiven those that have sinned against us. I remember watching a documentary about those responsible for taking the lives of innocent children in Greater Manchester in the 1960's. Truly shocking crimes. One victim was Lesley Ann Downey. My dad actually knew her older brother when he was a teenager. Anyway, the documentary focused on the lives of the families, and how they were coping with their lost. Lesley's mother, Mrs Ann West said: "I say the Lord's Prayer every night, but when it comes to the bit "Forgive us our sins as we forgive those that sin against us, I cannot say it." That poor lady, years later died full of torment and distress because she did not give it all to Almighty God for Him to deal with. Remember Almighty God will not violate free will either to those that carry out evil deeds or the victims of it, only on certain occasions like with the Japanese soldier that you will read about soon.

Nothing escapes Almighty God, and no one gets away with anything especially doing evil, each of us will give an account to Almighty God alone, but the way to Heaven has been made right because Our Lord Jesus put it right. We need to accept this free gift.

The warnings from Pope Francis in 2014

Our Holy Father Pope Francis warned the members of the mafia to… "Change their evil ways, to repent from their sins, and do good…" because if they continue they will end up in hell!"

This is a very strong warning message, but there is still time for people to change. The question is: are people willing to change? Hell is only around the corner, and not just for members of the mafia or gangs. Those that push drugs, beat women up, traffic men, women and children and have them abused, already have one foot in hell fire. But if they wish they can change their evil ways. Almighty God however will not violate free will. It is our responsibility to change, whether people are spending all the family finances getting drunk instead of feeding the family or people have proud hearts looking down on others less fortunate – sin is sin and each of us can sin through thoughts, words, deeds and omission (failing to do something). At the centre of our lives must be the Lord Jesus Christ. In Romans 5:17 it says, : " For if by one man's offence (Adam), death reigned by one; much more they which receive abundance of grace and the gift of righteousness shall reign in life by one, Jesus Christ. Those who receive Christ as their Lord and Saviour by faith through His grace (undeserving reward), they are clothed with Christ's own righteousness. We have a duty to forgive.

This is why the world is in such a terrible state because He is not at the centre of people's lives, but only a percentage. I heard on the radio in November 2014 that the most popular song to be played at a deceased's funeral is: "My Way," not God's way. My Way is a song I often sing at karaoke, but I change the words to God's Way or dedicate it to my mam and sing, mam's way. Pope Francis also reminds us to be careful how we use our free speech, and to be mindful about offending and ridiculing others. The only time we should look down on anyone is when we are helping them up.

Vocations to the Priesthood and Religious Life

The lack of clergy and religious is a cause for concern today. The devil has worked through the scandal and corruption. We are asked to pray regularly for an increase in vocations. Almighty God has answered prayers and sent men and women to live this lifestyle of service, however many have not been accepted. In the last ten years or so, I have heard about seminaries that have close down, and religious orders vacate houses and move out because they have so few numbers, but the penny has not dropped why this is happening. It is not because man and woman do not love Almighty God or not interested in that way of life. It is because I think those who are in charge are not neutering enough and in many cases trying to control the spirit of a person. In my case, I was going against the grain. I did not have any particular problems with my superiors, although there was a few I did not warm to - personality clashes, some have the power to love and some love the power. I just got on with it, but many I knew did voice issues especially those with strong and outspoken personalities, and there were a few of them. There was a kind of dictatorship instead of order and structure in the seminary at times, I am sad to say - when and how you will pray, when you will study, eat, and socialise, too full on for some people that prefer their own company. This is why we have the situation we do, who would want to live like that, in a sense being dictated to? Superiors can be too rigid. There is a difference between guiding a formation and quenching the Spirit of Almighty God.

On one occasion, during our termly reports, all the students would discuss their progress with each other and support each other. I remember one superior wrote in a report that a student was overweight and he was asked to go on a diet. A fair comment you would say if he was grossly obese, but the superior was very obese himself! There was no surprise that particular student was discouraged by hypocrisy, and left the seminary. This is just one example of the treatment a student can experience in seminary life. On another occasion in a staff/seminarians house meeting, students had raised a concern that there was a lack of variety on the menu because sweetcorn was served nearly every dinner time. The answer the students got was they were told they should be grateful for what they get because millions in the world are starving! I know that the students, including me, did appreciate what food they had, and were not worrying about food like the Lord Jesus advises us (Matthew 6:25). I will come back to this piece of scripture. They were just raising a point. After all, their dioceses and religious orders were paying for their training. But for the students to be made to feel guilty, like they had sinned against Almighty God, was wrong. Because one is serving Almighty God does not mean they should be served sweetcorn all the time! I think you get the picture. I suggest for those entering training for the priesthood and religious life, to do so in a parish setting in order to serve the community, and study Theology at college. Placements in a variety of areas where needed – hospitals, prisons, schools etc. should also be included. Formation is an important process. Superiors need to be more like guardians than RSM'S! (Regimental Sergeant Majors). From my own personal experience it has been the unchurched that have been most helpful in times of crisis and need towards me. I know in my heart this is why Almighty God wishes for these people to accept Him because they are carrying out His will without even realising it, daily living the life of a Good Samaritan. Our Lord Jesus informed those present, listening to Him teach

(Luke 10:25-37), which of the three people were right with Almighty God as each encountered a badly beaten man, a victim of a robbery? It was not the holy priest or the Levite that did Almighty's God holy will, but a Samaritan. The Samaritan demonstrated what loving our neighbour all is about, not just talking the talk, but love in action, the second greatest commandment fulfilled here – "Love thy neighbour." Our Lord Jesus also warns the proud and conceited that others that they deem to be beneath them in life, might get to the kingdom of heaven before they do. (Matthew 21:31). Almighty God wants a personal relationship with what the world would say lesser people. This is why He called ordinary people at first and still does. His mercy is great and open to everyone in His Divine Mercy as you will read about shortly. Saint Faustina received very little education, yet the Lord Jesus chose her personally to be His Secretary of His Divine Mercy.

Hope

As I have heard it often said as I have aged, "Be careful what you hope and wish for." This may have some truth, however where Almighty God is concerned this is exactly what one does all the time that loves Him, hope and wish. I am a witness that all prayers are answered, not always in our time or the way we expect either. We are called to trust in Almighty God in all circumstances. **Have I not commanded you? Be strong and courageous. Do not be terrified; do not be discouraged, for the LORD your God will be with you wherever you go." Joshua 1:9. O LORD Almighty, blessed is the man who trusts in you. Psalm 84:12. "Do not let your hearts be troubled. Trust in God; trust also in me. John 14:1.** These words were directly spoken by our Lord Jesus, and often spoken by the priest at a funeral to those in grief. I have been to my fair share of funerals, often paying respects to people I never knew. Within a short time, it is evident to me whether the family of the deceased are practising or not because the priest literally needs to guide them through the service, when the congregation to kneel and when to stand up etc. Their faith is known to Almighty God alone.

There have been many that are inconsolable at their loss. For them and for you dear reader if you are one of those people, Almighty God says this through His fearless preacher the Apostle St. Paul: **"If God is for us, who can ever be against us? Since He did not spare even His own Son but gave him up for us all, will He also give us everything else? Who dares accuse us whom God has chosen for His own? No one—for God himself has given us right standing with himself. Who then will condemn us? No one— for Christ Jesus died for us and was raised to life for us, and he is sitting in the place of honour at God's right hand, pleading for us.**

Can anything ever separate us from Christ's love? Does it mean he no longer loves us if we have trouble or calamity, or are persecuted, or hungry, or destitute, or in danger, or threatened with death? "For your sake we are killed every day; we are being slaughtered like sheep."**[No, despite all these things, overwhelming victory is ours through Christ, who loved us.**

And I am convinced that nothing can ever separate us from God's love. Neither death nor life, neither angels nor demons, neither our fears for today nor our worries about tomorrow—not even the powers of hell can separate us from God's love. No power in the sky above or in the earth below—indeed, nothing in all creation will ever be able to separate us from the love of God that is revealed in Christ Jesus our Lord. Romans 8:31-39. What more reassurances do we need? Absolutely nothing in our existence can separate us from the love of Almighty God, but we all must accept it. Sadly many do not believe in these assurances from Almighty God or many have given up when the going has gotten tough or for whatever the reason. Many people say: "I do not need to go to church." What about walking with those that do in faith? As communities, we need to build each other up and be there for each other.

Dear Reader, I do not consider myself as a preacher, but I have felt inspired to write, but like what I said in the beginning of this book, my job is to make the Lord Jesus Christ known, and that you, the reader, will get to know Him personally, then also make Him known to others. The world is so needy of the Lord Jesus Christ.

The Divine Mercy of the Lord Jesus Christ

If you are one of these people that do not know Almighty God and or you are separated from Him, all can be put right. You can give your life to Almighty God right now through His only begotten Son Jesus who died in your place on the cross.

You can make this commitment or renewal of faith today. The Lord Jesus died so that the friendship between His Father and us could be restored. If you have not bothered about the Lord Jesus, you can come back to Him through your heart. You can do this just as you are even if you do not feel very happy or if things in life are not going well, the Lord Jesus knows everything about you and will help you. I once heard that if we take 1 step towards the Lord Jesus, He takes 10 steps towards us. How wonderful Almighty God is!

The following prayer is The Miracle Prayer. It's exactly that – A Miracle. Jesus works miracles through this prayer for those that say it from the heart and with the right intentions, (He has with me, and not just for the lottery win, like I requested!)

Please say this prayer quietly to the Lord Jesus who is listening to you and mean it from your heart:

Lord Jesus, I come before you, just as I am. I am sorry for my sins (wrongdoings), I repent of my sins. Please forgive me. In your name, I forgive all others for what they have done against me. I renounce Satan, the evil spirits and all their works. I give you my entire self.

Lord Jesus, now and forever, I invite you into my life Jesus. I accept you as my Lord, God and Saviour. Heal me, change me, and strengthen me in body, soul and spirit.

Come Lord Jesus, cover me with your precious blood, and fill me with your Holy Spirit / I Love You Lord Jesus / I Praise You Jesus / I Thank

You Jesus / I shall follow you every day of my life. Amen.

Mary my Mother, Queen of Peace, all the Angels and Saints, please help me. Amen.

The Divine Mercy of the Lord Jesus Christ is the last warning for all mankind. If the world refuses His mercy, the world will receive His justice. The Divine Mercy is a ticket to heaven despite one's past life of sinfulness. The invitation from Jesus is overwhelming that He said: **"The worse the sinner; the greater access one has to my mercy."** What great assurance from Jesus to us all.

We are all sinners and we have all fallen short of Almighty God's perfect standards. As sinners we can never meet what God requires from us by ourselves. That is why God's Son the Lord Jesus Christ needed to die for us and pay the price. He cancelled our debt for those who accept Him in faith. Our Lord Jesus Christ is pleading to all mankind to turn from their sins with childlike trust to Him – today. The Lord Jesus does not promise an easy life, but He promises that all who give their lives to Him, live for Him and accept His mercy which is held from no one, will receive great mercy, unimaginable graces from Him and eternal life after death. The life is short and we have temporary needs.

The Secretary of the Divine Mercy is St. Faustina (1905-1938). St. Faustina was a simple, humble nun with a great love and devotion to Jesus. St. Faustina, like so many others has lived their lives in, and for the service of Almighty God and neighbour. Saint Faustina was specially chosen by Jesus to be the Secretary of His Divine Mercy, this is offered to everyone.

This is what you (the reader) and I are called to do at the beginning of each new day by offering ourselves, our intentions, and prayers for Almighty God's service.

St. Faustina heard and accepted the call from the Lord Jesus, will you? How long will the human race ignore and put off Almighty God's calling?

I pray dear reader that you do not ignore Almighty God, yet come to know Him personally, and make Him known to others.

The Lord Jesus Christ, bled and died for you and me because of our sins. This shows how precious the human race is to Almighty God that He would have His only begotten Son to die for us. Almighty

God has no need of our prayers or worship but this is His wonderful gift to us and we are united to Him our creator.

Saint Faustina (1905-1938) Divine Mercy Apostle

St. Faustina was born Helena Kowalska on 25th
August 1905, in the village of Glogowiec in Poland.
She was the third of ten children. Her parents were
poor but they taught their children the love of
Almighty God, and respect for other people.
Helena's whole life was characterised by those
virtues. When Helena was twenty years old, she
entered the apostolic congregation of the Sisters of
Our Lady of Mercy, here she worked hard and lived
a humble life. Helena distinguished herself by a
special devotion to Divine Mercy and trust in Jesus

which she endeavoured to bring to all who came to know her.

Jesus I Trust in You!

Dear reader please read about the Life and Times of Sister Faustina. Saint Faustina had a vision on 22nd February 1931 of the Our Jesus dressed in a white robe, and heard these words from Him:

"Paint an image of the picture you see, with the words, Jesus I Trust in You. I desire this image to be venerated and blessed on the first Sunday after Easter. This is to be the Feast of Mercy. Many artists attempted to draw from Sister Faustina's instructions as to what the Lord Jesus looked like in her vision, but she was not happy with any of the paintings and cried because the painting was not as beautiful as the vision she had seen of the Lord. The Lord told Sister Faustina that neither is it in the ability of the artist or in the beauty of the colour to have it exactly like He is. The image is to give us a better focus on our Lord Jesus especially the significance of the blood and water rays from His divine heart. The water cleanses the soul and the blood gives new life to the soul. Saint Faustina also kept a spiritual diary; here are some of the things our Lord said to her:

"My mercy is greater than your sins and those of the entire world. Who can measure the extent of my goodness? For you I descended from heaven to earth; for you I allowed myself to be nailed to the cross; for you I let my Sacred Heart be pierced with a lance, thus opening wide the source of mercy for you."

On another occasion the Lord Jesus instructed St. Faustina to write in her diary:

"Before I come as a Just Judge, I am coming first as the King of Mercy. Before the day of justice arrives, there will be given to people a sign in the heavens of this sort: All light in the heavens will be extinguished, and there will be darkness over the whole earth. Then the sign of the cross will be seen in the sky, and from the openings, where the hands and feet of the saviour were nailed will come forth great lights which will light up the earth for a period of time. This will take place shortly before the last day."

The Lord Jesus has shown through His chosen Secretary and Apostle of His Divine Mercy St. Faustina, the great urgency for all peoples to believe in Him and trust His mercy. At the hour of a person's death our Lord promises that if a person at the dying person's bedside says the Eternal Father prayer, the dying person will be granted abundant mercy. These are the words our Lord Jesus gave to Sister Faustina: **" Eternal Father, I offer you the body, blood, soul and divinity of your dearly beloved son our Lord Jesus Christ in atonement of our sins and for the sins of the whole world, for the sake of his sorrowful passion have mercy on us and on the whole**

world. " On one occasion Sister Faustina had a vision of an angel of Almighty God ready to strike a certain place because of its sinfulness. As Sister Faustina recited the Eternal Father prayer the angel disappeared. Just as in the first century with His first Apostles with the great urgency to go and make disciples of all the nations (Matthew 28:19) so it is today. We all must make that choice, accept Him and His mercy for all of us, be granted eternity with Him in His Kingdom or eternity without Him.

So many people today are distracted by the devil and the world's media. So many people prefer to put worldly possessions, status, power, and passion; to name a few things at the centre of their lives instead of Christ being the centre of their lives. The Lord Jesus said that: "**I am the way, the truth and the life. No one goes to the father accept by me**." (John 14:6). The Lord Jesus is directly informing us that not all roads lead to Almighty God despite other faiths having their values, He is the only way. Everyone must come through THE Lord Jesus and no one else. Our Blessed Lady, St. Joseph, and all the saints focus themselves and us on the Lord Jesus.

Isaiah 55:6-9

Seek the LORD while you can find him.
Call on him now while he is near.
Let the wicked change their ways
and banish the very thought of doing wrong.

Let them turn to the LORD that he may have mercy on them. Yes, turn to our God, for he will forgive generously.

"My thoughts are nothing like your thoughts," says the LORD. "And my ways are far beyond anything you could imagine.

For just as the heavens are higher than the earth, so my ways are higher than your ways and my thoughts higher than your thoughts.

There are two main reasons for people denying Christ in their lives. Firstly, one is what I have touched on - people would rather live their own way than the way Christ commands them to. By making this decision, people put other things at the centre of their lives. There is no prayer and no communication with Almighty God, unless people are in trouble and need help, "Oh my God, help with this or that." I struggle to think how Almighty God must feel being treated just as an emergency service, and only contacted when someone wants something or bailing out! Yes, they are relying on Almighty God, rather than their own strength, but our motive for prayer should not be in need, want or desire. We pray in thanksgiving and to give all the glory to Him. Sadly, people develop inflexibility with Almighty God's will, and put their own will first. Generally people will claim to believe in Almighty God, and hedge their bets, marrying in church, getting their kids Christened, might be done unreservedly for a school place and a party afterwards. This is what I mean about the wrong motive. Of course people attend funerals. Is this genuinely because the deceased person's soul is being remembered by Almighty God from the faithful or just part of the routine to be seen by others? Only Almighty God knows, but still it is mostly lukewarm service and Almighty God deserves more from us. Almighty God has called us by name and we are His (Isaiah 43:1). We must be willing and open in our hearts to Him who created us and loves us.

The truth is, for many people giving an hour a week on a Sunday including supporting their parish community is just too much trouble for them, even for the young and the fit and healthy. They are one hit wonders and the devil will put other tempting offers there for people to keep their minds from Almighty God. Of course, there is nothing wrong with having interests and activities outside church life, but if Christ is not at the centre of our lives this is wrong and will be a downfall. Almighty God commands that if we are true followers; He must come first (Luke 14:26). How do you answer Almighty God on judgement day, what are the excuses? All of us were told in Almighty God's holy word: **This day I call the heavens and the earth as witnesses against you that I**

have set before your life and death, blessings and curses. Now choose life...Deuteronomy 30:19. It is therefore better to act now and choose life while there is still time! I must add that the Government in this country and others will be held to account for taking the holy day of Sunday away too as well as other things!

Secondly, why people do not believe in the Lord Jesus is because He is reduced to being just a good man and a good teacher. This is despite Jesus on different occasions stating His Divinity (Equality with Almighty God). Jesus claimed to be on par with Almighty God and therefore: Divine. Let us pay some close attention to Jesus' claims about Himself being Almighty God. Let us never insult Him or short change Him therefore by saying He is just a good man or teacher. We do our Lord Jesus a disservice. Let us look carefully at what the Lord Jesus says concerning Himself.

The Lord Jesus said the following:

"My father goes on working and so do I" (John 5:17).

In the beginning was the word. And the word was with God; and the word was God (John1:1). Jesus was with His father before everything. Jesus is the word.

Jesus answered: "**You do not know me or my father; if you knew me, you would know my father as well**" (John 8:19).

Jesus said: "**You are from below and I am from above; you are from this world and I am not from this world. That is why I told you that you will die for your sins. And you shall die in your sins unless you believe that I am He**" (John 8:23).

And Jesus said: "**Truly, I say to you, before Abraham was, I am (God)** (John 8:57).

Jesus said: "**I and my Father are one**" (John 10:30).

Jesus said to Pilate: **"My Kingdom is not of this world..."** Pilate replied: "So, you are a king then?" Jesus answered: **"You say that I am a King, Yes, in fact, I was born for this reason, to testify to the truth."**

The Lord Jesus also allowed His followers to worship Him (Matthew 14:33 & Matthew 28:9). For a Jew; this would have been the ultimate sin and blasphemy; yet even as a baby, the wise men came to worship the new born king and present their gifts to Him (Matthew 2:2). Think about this for a moment; if Jesus was not Almighty God, and He allowed this worshipping of Himself to take place, He was not good at all. Those that witnessed Jesus' teachings and miracles however, reported that what Jesus said and did was reliable, rational and consistent. And not once does Jesus deny who He is even to the point of His death. Anyone lying about such a claim to be God at that point would no doubt hold their hands up and say "Ok, you have sussed me; I do not want to die, I was joking!" The Lord Jesus does not say this. We should be mindful that as well as being totally divine, the Lord Jesus was also fully human. He asks His Father that if there is any other way other than what He must go through; let it happen instead, but at all times asking that the will of His Father be done.

(Mark 14:36). There is no other way. Jesus makes the ultimate sacrifice in our place. For me, this demonstrates just how much Almighty God loves us and just how much we need the Lord Jesus if we want to get to heaven. Despite the Lord's death, resurrection and ascension into heaven, this has not been enough for many people. We must not insult the Lord Jesus by referring to Him as just a good man, but give Him heartfelt praise as He is Almighty God.

(John14.6) Jesus answered: "I am the way, the truth and the life. No one comes to the Father except through me.

The Lord Jesus said to Saint Faustina:

"Here the misery of the soul meets the God of mercy. Tell souls that from this fount of mercy souls draw graces solely with the vessel of trust. If their trust is great, there is no limit to my generosity. The torrents of grace inundate humble souls. The proud remain always in poverty and misery, because My grace turns away from them to humble souls."

The Lord Jesus went on to tell St. Faustina that even though He had done all these things, people still ignored Him and His teachings. The Lord Jesus works through different people and in different ways. Ways they understand and can relate to. It is important for me to write that not all ways of living give Glory to Almighty God, and people must choose the path they will walk on. If every way of living was acceptable, Almighty God's word would not be necessary and it would be a free for all according to one's own view of what is right. Despite God being Almighty, there is one thing we know He cannot do – tell lies. The Lord Jesus says He came to fulfill the law and not abolish it (Matthew 5:17). For any human being to say that there is not a God, would mean that they would need to be everywhere and know everything. We know that no human being can be everywhere at the same time and no human being can know everything. The time to accept and believe Jesus is now, do not delay! He is very gracious and kind.

Parable of the Vineyard Workers

Matthew 20.1-16
"For the Kingdom of Heaven is like the landowner who went out early one morning to hire workers for his vineyard. He agreed to pay the normal daily wage and sent them out to work. "At nine o'clock in the morning he was passing through the market place and saw some people standing around doing nothing. So he hired them, telling them he would pay them whatever was right at the end of the day. So they went to work in the vineyard. At noon and again at three o'clock he did the same thing.

"At five o'clock that afternoon he was in town again and saw some more people standing around. He asked them, "Why haven't you been working today?" "They replied, "Because no one hired us.""

"The landowner told them, then go out and join the others in my vineyard."

"That evening he told the foreman to call the workers in and pay them, beginning with the last workers first. When those hired at five o'clock were paid, each received a full day's wage. When those hired first came to get their pay, they assumed they would receive more. But they, too, were paid a day's wage. When they received their pay, they protested to the owner, "those people worked only one hour, and yet you've paid them just as much as you paid us who worked all day in the scorching heat.""

"He answered one of them, "Friend, I haven't been unfair! Didn't you agree to work all day for the usual wage? Take your money and go. I wanted to pay this last worker the same as you. Is it against the law for me to do what I want with my money? Should you be jealous because I am kind to others?" "So those who are last now will be first then, and those who are first will be last.""

If we reflect on this parable of the Vineyard Workers, we could feel hard done by if we have put in all the work to serve Jesus and build up His kingdom. Someone comes along for a short time, does only a little work yet receives the same reward. This shows us how wonderfully generous and giving Almighty God is. He is the best employer

168

we could ever have. That is why I said do not delay! Grasp the prize with both hands and never let go.

Music, television and its influence

Almighty God works through our emotions. He works through music and television. How many of us can say that they are really moved by a particular song or movie that makes us happy? This is great, and the artist has developed their talents given to them by Almighty God. There is however a lot of bad influences in the world today, and I feel I am inspired to alert you. There is a great threat to the minds of young people, in particular, the content of a lot of, shall we say, unsavoury music and television shows. As adults we have a responsibility to protect our young people from this influence to their minds. If you are an adult and are following this trend, please pray about this for the protection of the young people around you that could be affected by these bad influences. If you are a young person; please pray and reflect about the bad taste that some music, films, and television shows contain if this is affecting your life and your new life with the Lord Jesus (if you have accepted Him).

Idolatry and materialism

This continues to be a big concern in our world today. Whether the idol is greed for more and more excess, even though we may have too much already, watching and idolising filth or through pride comparing and looking down on a less well-off person, this is all sinful towards Almighty God. The only time we should look down on anyone is when we are helping them up. The Lord Jesus told a story to a crowd: **"The ground of a certain rich man yielded an abundant harvest. He thought to himself: What should I do? I have nowhere to store my crops. Then he said: "This is what I will do, I will tear down my barns and build bigger ones, and there I will store my surplus grain." And I will say to myself: "You have plenty of grain laid up for many years, take life easy; eat, drink and be merry." But God said to him: "You fool! This very night your life will be demanded from you. Then who will get what you have prepared for yourself?"** (Luke 12:21).

The message of the Lord Jesus here is not that having nice things is a bad thing, but ultimately our riches will leave us or we will leave our riches behind when we die. There are no pockets in shrouds as the saying goes. The centre of our lives must never be our excessive grain from the crops, our surplus money, houses, cars, social status etc. If the idol, whatever it is, takes the place of Him who died for us, this is not pleasing to Him. The Lord Jesus goes on to say: **"Do not be anxious about your life, what you will eat or drink; or about your body what you will wear. Is not life more than food and the body more than clothes?"** (Matthew 6:25)

How many in this day and age live life anxiously? Many I would say, and the pressures of life are getting worse. We have a state of cathedrals of consumerism. The media are waving the red flag, people are pressurised to have the best of anything until something better comes along and then it is no longer the best. It never ends. We have a society that can never give fulfilment with materialism. There is no lasting fulfilment in materialism.

It goes without saying, if the leaders of the nations paid heed to Holy Scripture, the world would be a better place for all. There would be no poverty or social injustice. There are many people in the world that follow the Lord Jesus today that are paying the price with losing their jobs, families, friends, and even with their lives because they refuse to deny and denounce their faith in the Lord Jesus. It was not just under Henry VIII that people suffered because of their faith. Being a Christian makes you different. Christians are different, living in the world but not of it. I have never wanted to be of this world. The fact is anyone that loves the Lord Jesus will be hated by the devil and all those that work for the devil. I do not like giving the devil any attention but you should know that there are many millions in the world today offering themselves to Satan and his service. One of the jobs for the Satanist is to attend holy mass and steal the sacred body and blood of the Lord Jesus for their black mass. The Lord Jesus permits Himself to be treated in this way in sacrament. We know He will never die again, but I often wonder why He permits this against Himself. No doubt we will know when we meet Him.

I remember once my Godfather Albert telling me a story from the Second World War when some Japanese soldiers entering a church in Malaysia with guns when some people including nuns were praying. A soldier demanded what the people were doing, and a lady replied: "We are praying to Jesus. He is present in His tabernacle." The soldier did not understand their language or what they were doing, he was angry, and pointed his rifle at the Lord Jesus in the tabernacle taking aim to fire. As he was about to pull the trigger, that soldier dropped to the floor and died instantly. It was a mystery and so remains a mystery. Also present in the church was a Japanese army officer. He witnessed this, and gave a full account of the events.

The Holy Sacrament is always real and present. Our Lord Jesus promised us all that He will be with us always, yes even to the end of time (Matthew 28:20). The Sacrifice of the Holy Mass is the same Sacrifice on Calvary made present through the power of the Holy Spirit and the words of institution spoken by the priest for our time. Our Lord Jesus' sacrifice on the cross was/is an Eternal Sacrifice and is valid for all time for the forgiveness of all sins. The Lord Jesus was and is in Heaven, but in His sacraments with His Holy Spirit. He is on earth, and should always be adored until He returns again. I believe that the Japanese soldier was struck down. Only the Lord knows what punishment that man would have had to endure if he had been permitted to fire at Him in the Tabernacle. Always show reverence in any Catholic Church before Our Lord Jesus in His Tabernacle.

Today, just like in history, in many parts of the world there are people that are spiritually and psychically under attack, and carry their cross every day, suffering like the Lord Jesus. We must pray for all of them as they unite their sufferings with the Lord Jesus. Please pray for the conversion of sinners as we have been instructed to do in the Divine Mercy.

The rewards of eternal life wait for us up there because one certainly does not always get the rewards justice down here! Life is not always fair, but it will not always be this way. The Lord Jesus has come off the cross for those that accept Him and love Him, yet He remains on the cross for those that reject and refuse Him.

The Lord Jesus continues to bless my family and myself in His Divine Mercy. Thanks Lord Jesus.

My youngest brother Trevor was married to Marie on 25th July 2014. Trevor, as I have mentioned is my youngest brother. When he left school he served in the British Army for 6 years. Trevor's faith in Jesus has been a massive help to him. The Lord Jesus never promised His followers an easy, trouble free life, but we will all be complete when we are with the Lord Jesus Himself.

Trevor met Marie in 2012. Trevor was baptised and fully received into the Roman Catholic Church on Wednesday 23rd July 2014. My wife and I were very honoured to be his sponsors.

Trevor and Marie were married on 25th July 2014 at St. Marie's R.C Church in Bury, Greater Manchester. St. Marie's parish was where the Xaverian Brothers came to first from Belgium, to provide free education to the poor people in Manchester in the 1800's.

Like me, Trevor had decided that he wanted both Paul and me to be his best men. Our Paul would look after their wedding rings, and I would be involved with the liturgy and give the best man's speech. I was again very honoured as I was at Paul's wedding back in 2003.

We could not have asked for a better day, praise to Almighty God for prayers answered. The sun was shining, and no rain. The whole celebration could not have gone any better

After the beautiful ceremony and Holy Mass, we all gathered in the church grounds for some photos. We were so blessed with great weather. Soon after, we enjoyed a meal at Bury Town Hall. I was honoured to speak again in the capacity of the best man. It was a very proud moment for me and I spoke from my heart.

The evening was soon upon us and more relatives and friends joined in the celebrations. We enjoyed a lovely buffet and a disco. I will never forget this wonderful occasion.

On 31st October 2015, Trevor and Marie became the proud parents of Wyatt Joseph Walker. I became his Godparent, very honoured. Thanks be to Almighty God for ensuring it went so well.

May Almighty God bless them and all my family, friends, relatives, relations, and all those known to me. We will continue to spread His Divine Mercy with joy and love.

To date, I continue to work at Xaverian College, Almighty God brought me here. I would not be able to do my daily job without Him looking after me and being with me, and I would not want to do the job without Almighty God. It is only possible with His unfailing help. Almighty God has been so gracious to me and given me all the wonderful gifts of His Holy Spirit to help me, help others, and use for the Glory of His Kingdom. He has also given me the gift of discerning of spirits (especially with strangers) and the gift of tongues.

At every opportunity, spend time with the Lord Jesus in His house. In silent meditation, close your eyes. As you breathe in say in your mind: "My Lord Jesus." And when you breathe out say in your mind: "I love you." The Lord Jesus will bless you abundantly and fill your being with peace.

Dear Reader, please commit to memory the bible verses below and meditate on them. The Bible provides every answer and gives reassurances the world could never give us. We are to trust in Almighty God's unlimited mercy and goodness to us.

We are called to have the correct concept for prayer, speak to Father God and give Him all the glory, offer back to Him in love the greatest person He gave us to die for us, His only begotten son Jesus our Lord and saviour.

Matthew 6:33: "Seek first the kingdom of God and His righteousness and all these things will be added to you." It is my prayer for you the reader.

"For those with faith in God, no explanation is ever necessary. For those with no faith in God, no explanation is possible." I pray you will believe in and have faith in God.

"God please grant us the serenity to accept the things we cannot change, courage to change the things we can, and the wisdom to know the difference."

Morning Offering to Jesus

Lord Jesus, I love you, and I always will. When I wake each morning I think of you still. Today I surrender to do as you will whatever you plan Lord I willingly do.

Eternal Father my soul possess, to see your creation in all that I view, thank you my father for letting me be brother to Jesus in your family.

Almighty God Holy Spirit, re-kindle in me the gifts you gave me in life to endure, of love, understanding, wisdom and hope to help me to serve you in people today.

Mary my Queen and mother, please over ride, in your special way all my prayers and intentions of this day.

Almighty God, I consecrate to you my life, my family and all those known to me to your divine care.

Through Jesus Christ my Lord

Amen

Night prayer

Almighty God, thank you for all the benefits and blessings of this day. Please forgive any sins I may have committed. As I rest, please be close to my heart and look after me during the night so I will awake refreshed and ready to serve you in a brand new day.

Through Jesus Christ my Lord

Amen

I have always been a great sleeper, but only when I have said my night prayers, otherwise I cannot settle, strange it is? It is as if my angel will not let me switch off! Almighty God does not mind what posture you are in, kneeling at the side of your bed or with your head on your pillow, what matters is what is in your heart and being thankful to Him. Sadly many forget this and end the day as if Almighty God is not there!

The Holy Rosary

MYSTERIES OF THE ROSARY			
JOYFUL	LUMINOUS	SORROWFUL	GLORIOUS
Mondays & Saturdays and Sundays of Advent	Thursdays	Tuesdays & Fridays Sundays of Lent	Wednesdays & Sundays
1. The Annunciation 2. The Visitation 3. The Nativity 4. The Presentation 5. Finding of Jesus in the Temple	1. Baptism in the Jordan 2. Wedding at Cana 3. Proclamation of the Kingdom of God 4. Transfiguration 5. Institution of the Eucharist	1. Agony in the Garden 2. Scourging at the Pillar 3. Crowning with Thorns 4. Carrying of the Cross 5. Crucifixion	1. The Resurrection 2. The Ascension 3. Descent of the Holy Spirit 4. The Assumption 5. The Coronation
THINK OF ONE MYSTERY WHILE SAYING A COMPLETE DECADE			

An opportunity for quiet prayer and reflection, meditating on the life of the Lord Jesus from the Annunciation that He was to be born to save the world from sin, to Him crowning His and our Mother

Mary in Heaven. The Holy Rosary can be a difficult way of praying for some, and it does require some concentration. If the Holy Rosary is said at night some people fall asleep holding their rosary, but do not worry about it if you do, Almighty God does not love us any less! The rosary and pictures are prayer aids to assist us meditating.

Simply requesting the support of Our Lady and by meditating on the Lord Jesus' earthly life is praying; just bring your intentions and concerns from your heart to Him through each mystery.

Mother Mary is closer to Jesus than we have ever been. Mother Mary is most precious to Him, chosen for Him by God the Father before all time. Mother Mary carried Him, gave birth to Him and looked after Him. Each of the meditations represents a beautiful flower being given to Our Lady. This is very pleasing to Our Lord Jesus, just as it would be if someone gave our mothers some flowers.

It was also Mary's role with the power of the Holy Spirit, when the Lord Jesus went to heaven to build and support His first followers. She has always done this through the ages. We know that our Lord Jesus would never refuse His mam anything. Mary no longer needs to hope to Jesus like she hoped He would be okay when she thought He was missing in the temple as a child (Luke 2:41-52).

Mother Mary does however get upset with the way the world is and she hopes and pleads for people to change and give their lives to Her Son.

I know that she has forgiven me for requesting the six winning Lotto numbers! I will never ask her again for such a selfish request. I will never ignore her and request that you dear reader, never ignore her either!

Stations of the Cross

This is a very meditative way of praying and is usually said in a group but can be meditated upon individually. Each station recalls the punishment Our Lord Jesus endured for each of us.

Opening Prayer

ACT OF CONTRITION

O my God, my Redeemer, behold me here at Thy feet. From the bottom of my heart I am sorry for all my sins, because by them I have offended Thee, Who art infinitely good. I will die rather than offend thee again.

Before each station the following is said:

We adore you O' Christ and bless thee (you). Because by your holy cross Thou (you) have redeemed the world.

1. The Lord Jesus is condemned to death.

2. The Lord Jesus carries his cross.

3. The Lord Jesus falls the first time.

4. The Lord Jesus meets his mother.

5. Simon of Cyrene helps the Lord Jesus carry the cross.

6. Veronica wipes the face of Jesus.

7. The Lord Jesus falls the second time.

8. The Lord Jesus meets the women of Jerusalem.

9. The Lord Jesus falls the third time.

10. The Lord Jesus is stripped of his garments.

11. Crucifixion: The Lord Jesus is nailed to the cross.

12. The Lord Jesus dies on the cross.

13. The Lord Jesus is taken down from the cross. (Deposition or Lamentation)

14. The Lord Jesus is laid in the tomb.

Like the Holy Rosary, the Stations of the Cross for readers that do not know is a prayerful scriptural meditation that focuses on the passion journey of our Lord Jesus from His agony in the garden to Him being laid in the tomb. There is not an Easter Sunday without a Good Friday!

Remember that before our Lord Jesus rose from the dead victorious over sin, Satan and death on that first Easter Sunday; He went through so much for you and me to put things right with His father and our father. Let us always be mindful, thankful and grateful to Almighty God for His Divine Mercy.

The Divine Praises

Blessed be God.

Blessed be His Holy Name.

Blessed be Jesus Christ, true God and true man.

Blessed be His Most Sacred Heart.

Blessed be His Most Precious Blood.

Blessed be Jesus in the Most Holy Sacrament of the Altar.

Blessed be the Holy Spirit, the Paraclete.

Blessed be the great Mother of God, Mary most Holy.

Blessed be her Holy and Immaculate Conception.

Blessed be her Glorious Assumption.

Blessed be the name of Mary, Virgin and Mother.

Blessed be St. Joseph, her most chaste spouse.

Blessed be God in His Angels and in His Saints. Amen.

The Litany of the Sacred Heart of Jesus

Lord, have mercy on us.
Christ, have mercy on us.
Lord, have mercy on us. Christ, hear us.
Christ, graciously hear us.
God the Father of Heaven, *have mercy on us.*

(Repeat *have mercy on us.* after each line)
God the Son, Redeemer of the world,
God the Holy Spirit,
Holy Trinity, one God,
Heart of Jesus, Son of the Eternal Father,
Heart of Jesus, formed by the Holy Spirit in the Virgin Mother's womb,
Heart of Jesus, substantially united to the Word of God,
Heart of Jesus, of infinite majesty,
Heart of Jesus, holy temple of God,
Heart of Jesus, tabernacle of the Most High,
Heart of Jesus, house of God and gate of heaven,
Heart of Jesus, glowing furnace of charity,

Heart of Jesus, vessel of justice and love,
Heart of Jesus, full of goodness and love,
Heart of Jesus, abyss of all virtues,
Heart of Jesus, most worthy of all praise,
Heart of Jesus, King and centre of all hearts,
Heart of Jesus, in whom are all the treasures
of wisdom and knowledge,
Heart of Jesus, in whom dwells all the fullness of
the Godhead,
Heart of Jesus, in whom the Father was well
pleased,
Heart of Jesus, of whose fullness we have all
received,
Heart of Jesus, desire of the everlasting hills,
Heart of Jesus, patient and rich in mercy,
Heart of Jesus, rich to all who call upon You,
Heart of Jesus, fount of life and holiness,
Heart of Jesus, propitiation for our offences,
Heart of Jesus, overwhelmed with reproaches,
Heart of Jesus, bruised for our iniquities,
Heart of Jesus, obedient even unto death,
Heart of Jesus, pierced with a lance,
Heart of Jesus, source of all consolation,
Heart of Jesus, our life and resurrection,
Heart of Jesus, our peace and reconciliation,
Heart of Jesus, victim for our sins,
Heart of Jesus, salvation of those who hope in
You,
Heart of Jesus, hope of those who die in You,
Heart of Jesus, delight of all saints,
Lamb of God, who takes away the sins of the
world,
Spare us, O Lord.
Lamb of God, who takes away the sins of the
world,

Graciously hear us, O Lord.
Lamb of God, who takes away the sins of the world,
Have mercy on us.
Jesus, meek and humble of Heart,
Make our hearts like unto Thine.

Let us pray

Almighty and eternal God, look upon the Heart of Thy most beloved Son and upon the praises and satisfaction which He offers Thee in the name of sinners; and to those who implore Thy mercy, in Thy great goodness, grant forgiveness in the name of the same Jesus Christ, Thy Son,

who lives and reigns with Thee forever and ever. Amen.

Prayer after receiving our Lord Jesus at mass

Oh my Lord Jesus, I believe I have received your flesh to eat and your blood to drink because you have said it and you word is true. All that I am and all that I have are now your gift, now that you have given me yourself. Thank you Lord Jesus. Amen.

My Lord and My God

Trezelle's First Holy Communion

On the 19th October 2020, our Trezelle made her
first Holy Communion. May Almighty God bless her
now and always. We are so very proud of her.

189

Trezelle after receiving her first Holy Communion
with her certificate

Dear reader, it has been an honour and a privilege sharing Almighty God's great love with you. Thank you so much for reading this book. I hope you have enjoyed reading it as much as I have enjoyed writing it!

God bless you and yours,

Your friend Simon

simonwalker181173@yahoo.co.uk

It would be great to hear from you!

Royalties and donations from this publication are going to support children living in poverty.

Please be generous.

C/o Divine Mercy Prayer Group (Manchester)

Sort Code 11-66-87

Account Number 08404063

IBAN: GB71HLFX11668708404063

BIC: HLFXGB21Z10

Most Holy Trinity Have Mercy On Us

Glory be to the Father
Who by His Almighty Power and love created me,
making me in the image and likeness of God.

Glory be to the Son
Who by His Precious Blood delivered me from hell,
and opened for me the gates of heaven.

Glory be to the Holy Spirit
Who has sanctified me in the sacrament of
Baptism, and continues to sanctify me
by the graces I receive daily from His bounty.

Glory be to the Three adorable Persons of the Holy
Trinity now and forever. Amen.

Many thanks to all those who have loved and
supported me throughout my life so far.

God bless

Love

Simon

Printed in Great Britain
by Amazon

61411743R00112